Feasting on the Word®
WORSHIP COMPANION

ALSO AVAILABLE IN THIS SERIES

Feasting on the Word®
WORSHIP COMPANION

❧ LITURGIES FOR YEAR B ❧
VOLUME 1

EDITED BY

Kimberly Bracken Long

WESTMINSTER
JOHN KNOX PRESS
LOUISVILLE · KENTUCKY

© 2014 Westminster John Knox Press

First edition

Published by Westminster John Knox Press
Louisville, Kentucky

14 15 16 17 18 19 20 21 22 23—10 9 8 7 6 5 4 3 2 1

Book design by Drew Stevens
Cover design by Lisa Buckley and Dilu Nicholas

Library of Congress Cataloging-in-Publication Data

Feasting on the Word worship companion : liturgies for Year C / edited by Kimberly Bracken Long. — 1st ed.
   p. cm.
Includes index.
ISBN 978-0-664-23804-9 (Year B, v. 5 alk. paper)
ISBN 978-0-664-25962-4 (Year A, v. 4 alk. paper)
ISBN 978-0-664-23803-2 (Year A, v. 3 alk. paper)
ISBN 978-0-664-23918-3 (Year C, v. 2 alk. paper)
ISBN 978-0-664-23805-6 (Year C, v. 1 alk. paper)
  1. Common lectionary (1992) 2. Lectionaries. 3. Worship programs.
I. Long, Kimberly Bracken.
BV199.L42F43 2012
264'.13—dc23

                 2012011192

PRINTED IN THE UNITED STATES OF AMERICA

Most Westminster John Knox Press books are available at special quantity discounts when purchased in bulk by corporations, organizations, and special-interest groups. For more information, please e-mail SpecialSales@wjkbooks.com.

Contents

LENT

HOLY WEEK

EASTER

ADDITIONAL RESOURCES

Introduction

The *Feasting on the Word Worship Companion* offers language for the church's worship for every Sunday and holy day in the Revised Common Lectionary for Years A, B, and C. This volume provides liturgy for Year B, Advent through Pentecost. It is intended to serve as a supplement to the liturgical resources of denominations and not as a substitute for any of those fine works.

The texts herein were written by people from five ecclesial bodies who share similar convictions about worship and its language, yet pray with distinct voices. Because the writers come from a range of Protestant traditions, the attentive reader will notice some differences in theological background; in every case, however, these texts are grounded in deep and careful theological reflection. We seek to offer liturgy that is accessible yet elegant, in words that are poetic but not overwrought. These texts are written for the ear; we hope they are easily spoken, and their meanings quickly apprehended, in order to encourage full and rich congregational participation in the church's life of prayer.

These words are rooted in Scripture, as the church's liturgies have been for centuries. Using the Revised Common Lectionary as a guide, the writers of this volume offer words for worship that do not merely spring from their own imaginations but are grounded in the Word of God.

What This Book Includes

— Prayers and other liturgical texts—from Opening Words to Blessing— for every Sunday and holy day from Advent through Pentecost (Year B)
— A collection of greetings to be used at the beginning of a worship service

- Thanksgiving for Baptism, for use at the beginning of a worship service or for reaffirmation of baptism
- Prayers for Communion, or Eucharist
- Questions for reflection on the texts for each Sunday and holy day
- Morning and evening prayers for household use, to be prayed by individuals, families, or groups, based on the week's lectionary readings. (These prayers are written in both singular and plural, so adapt them as needed.) These may be distributed throughout a congregation for use during the week as a way to continue reflecting on the Sunday texts.
- A CD-ROM, which enables worship planners to copy text and paste it in the worship bulletin. Permission is granted to reprint individual prayers and liturgical texts for worship provided that the following notice is included: Reprinted by permission of Westminster John Knox Press from *Feasting on the Word*® *Worship Companion.* Copyright 2014.

Eucharistic prayers are provided in a separate section in acknowledgment that not all Christian churches celebrate the Lord's Supper every Sunday. In addition, one prayer for general use is provided along with prayers for holy days and seasons.

How to Use This Book

One may use this book in a variety of ways. You may use the texts just as they are, or you may adapt them for your context. While new texts are offered for each Sunday, there is value in repeating portions of liturgy so that people might become familiar with them. When worshipers are able to speak the same set of words over a period of time, they are not continually adjusting to new ideas and patterns of speech. You may, for example, use the same prayer of confession for a season, allowing the people to enter more deeply into that prayer over time.

Although a basic fourfold pattern of worship is used here, the elements of worship may not be arranged in the same way they appear in your own church's order of worship. This is not intended to privilege one tradition over another, but simply to arrange the elements in a way that will look familiar to many who use this book.

You will notice that these texts are arranged in "sense lines"—that is, they look more like poems than paragraphs. This is intentional. The eye can pick up phrases quickly, enabling worshipers to pray them with greater understanding. So, if you reproduce any of these texts, please retain the sense lines.

This layout on the page also helps leaders to better speak the texts so that they can actually proclaim (and not just read) the texts, while maintaining eye contact with worshipers.

In cases where a congregational response is used, instructions are often included that will allow the prayers to be led without printing them in their entirety.

This book is full of words. Worship, however, does not happen on a page. As you use these texts, do not just read them. Pray them. Spend time with the words and make them your own so that you may lead with authenticity, wisdom, and a true sense of prayer.

A Word about the Lectionary

During Ordinary Time, or the season after Pentecost, liturgy is provided for both the semicontinuous and complementary streams of the Revised Common Lectionary. Each of these tracks uses the same Epistle and Gospel reading, but the Old Testament and Psalm lections are different. The semi-continuous track allows congregations to read continually through a book of Scripture from week to week. In the complementary track, the Old Testament readings are chosen to relate to (or complement) the Gospel reading of the day. In both cases, the psalm is understood as a response to the Old Testament reading. Liturgical resources for the Season after Pentecost will appear in the second volume of each year in the lectionary cycle.

Since the numbering of the Sundays after Pentecost varies from year to year, the designation of "Proper" is used here, as it is in the *Feasting on the Word* commentaries. It can be confusing to navigate the various ways churches designate Sundays; a handy resource for viewing all those labels in one place can be found at http://lectionary.library.vanderbilt.edu/, a user-friendly site provided to the public by Vanderbilt University.

Different Voices: The Ecumenical Nature of the Project

Each writer comes to his or her task having been formed by a particular liturgical tradition. We are Methodist, Episcopal, United Church of Christ, African Methodist Episcopal, Presbyterian, and Lutheran, with a variety of backgrounds and experiences. Working as a team, we chose elements of worship that are common to all of us, as well as some elements that are particular to one church but not necessarily to another. Presbyterians, for instance, insist on including prayers of confession and prayers for illumination that invoke the Holy Spirit. Lutherans and Episcopalians expect a prayer for the day and include prayers for the departed in the intercessions. Lutherans also commonly use language about law and grace, and declarations of forgiveness sometimes refer to the ordination of the presider. These particularities were retained in order to preserve the ecumenical character of the book.

We use a variety of ways of praying but a consistent pattern of worship elements for each Sunday in the Christian year. Feel free to adapt the forms, change the words, or choose what is best suited for your context.

Who We Are

Just as this book is intended to serve as a companion to *Feasting on the Word: Preaching the Revised Common Lectionary,* we seek to be companions along the way with those of you who plan and lead worship.

The core team of writers includes:

Kimberly L. Clayton, Director of Contextual Education at Columbia Theological Seminary, Decatur, Georgia; Presbyterian Church (U.S.A.)

David Gambrell, Associate for Worship in the Office of Theology and Worship of the Presbyterian Church (U.S.A.), Louisville, Kentucky; Presbyterian Church (U.S.A.)

Daniel M. Geslin, Pastor of Union Congregational Church of Hancock, Hancock, Maine; United Church of Christ

Kimberly Bracken Long, Associate Professor of Worship, Columbia Theological Seminary, Decatur, Georgia; Presbyterian Church (U.S.A.)

L. Edward Phillips, Associate Professor of Worship and Liturgical Theology, Candler School of Theology, Atlanta, Georgia; United Methodist Church

Melinda Quivik, Liturgical Scholar, Houghton, Michigan; Evangelical Lutheran Church in America

Carol L. Wade, Dean of Christ Church Cathedral, Lexington, Kentucky; Episcopal Church

The generosity of many people has helped bring this work to fruition. David Maxwell, executive editor of Westminster John Knox Press, has provided gentle guidance, shown great wisdom, and shared his seemingly boundless good humor. David Dobson, editorial director of WJK, has offered constant support and encouragement. Columbia Theological Seminary provided meeting space, hospitality, and encouragement for the project.

No words are sufficient to describe the depth of God's grace or beautiful enough to address to the creator of the cosmos. We offer these words with the prayer that they might be useful to the church in enabling worshiping communities to stammer forth their thanks and praise.

Kimberly Bracken Long

First Sunday of Advent

Isaiah 64:1–9   1 Corinthians 1:3–9
Psalm 80:1–7, 17–19   Mark 13:24–37

OPENING WORDS / CALL TO WORSHIP
O that God would tear open the heavens
and come down!   *Isa. 64:1*
Of that day or hour, no one knows, only God.   *Mark 13:32*
Be alert! Keep awake!   *Mark 13:33, 37*
The time is drawing near:
The beginning of the good news of Jesus Christ,   *Mark 1:1*
the Son of God.

CALL TO CONFESSION
Like a faded, dry leaf that the wind blows away, *Isa. 64:6b*
our sins dry us up;
faded and brittle, we are carried off
by the wrongs we have done.
Yet God loves us still
and is able to restore and renew us
with the water of life.

PRAYER OF CONFESSION
God-with-us,
even in Advent,
we confess that you can seem far away.   *Isa. 64:5b, 7*
You are hidden when we need you near.
In our hurt, doubt, and fear,
we do not try to draw closer to you;
instead, we lash out—
against you, our neighbor, even those we love.

1

Forgive us, we pray, and come to save us! *Ps. 80:2–7*
Let your face shine until our tears are dried,
our sins are faded, and our hope is restored.
After all, we belong to you, *Isa. 64:8*
and in your hands, we can be made new.
In Jesus' name we pray. Amen.

[or]

Merciful God,
we confess that we become distracted, *Mark 13:33, 37*
even weary, in our discipleship.
We keep busy schedules; we rush about.
Captivated by technology,
seduced by the lure of consumer goods,
we do not remain alert to your divine presence
in our lives, in the church, in the world.
Make us better doorkeepers of our lives, *Mark 13:34*
watching for you attentively.
Awaken us to your surprising power and glory
and peace, *Mark 13:26*
so we do not miss how near you are to our
very own gates. *Mark 13:29*
Be gracious toward us, we pray,
until we are gathered, from the ends of earth *Mark 13:27*
to the ends of heaven,
into your embrace.
We pray in the name of Christ,
who was, and is, and is to come. Amen.

DECLARATION OF FORGIVENESS

The grace of God, given to us in Christ Jesus, *1 Cor. 1:4, 8*
strengthens us to the end
so that we may be blameless when Christ comes again.
Thanks be to God, who is faithful *1 Cor. 1:9*
and has called us into the fellowship of the Son,
Jesus Christ our Lord!

PRAYER OF THE DAY

God of power unexpected,
we want you to tear open the heavens and come down; *Isa. 64:1*
to make mountains quake, water boil, and stars to fall *Mark 13:25*
until all nations tremble at your presence! *Isa. 64:2b*

But you,
you will not perform according to our wants and whims.
Instead you come like the sound of sheer silence:
    Thin. Quiet.   *1 Kgs. 19:12*
Instead you are born among us as an infant.   *Luke 2:16*
Instead you show us how love is made
    perfect in weakness.   *2 Cor. 12:9*
So we will stay alert,   *Mark 13:33*
or at least we will try,
because we are your people   *Isa. 64:9c, 4c*
and there is no other God besides you. **Amen.**

PRAYER FOR ILLUMINATION

Gracious God,
heaven and earth will pass away,   *Mark 13:31*
but your words will not pass away:
Your Word stands forever.   *Isa. 40:8*
May our generation be attentive   *Mark 13:30*
so that, by the power of your Holy Spirit,
we remember your ways   *Isa. 64:5*
and gladly do right,
meeting you wherever and whenever you appear.   *Mark 13:35*
In Christ's name we pray. **Amen.**

PRAYERS OF INTERCESSION

God of power and glory,
we remember your awesome deeds across the ages—   *Isa. 64:3*
the times you saved us and brought us home.
Yet, we also remember times   *Isa. 64:7*
when we felt alone and afraid.
O God, we are your people,   *Isa. 64:8–9*
the work of your hand.
Look upon us with your shining face,   *Ps. 80:3, 7, 19*
especially in the time of need.

We pray for those who look to you for healing
    and hope . . .
those who are sick or recuperating from
    illness and injury . . .
those who are lonely and need companionship
    and care . . .

those for whom the holidays bring sorrow or pain . . .
those whose deep sadness overshadows joy.
Let your face shine upon us, O God.

We pray for people in need of restoration and reconciliation:
for those battling addictions and those in recovery . . .
for people estranged from those they love . . .
for someone lost in grief . . .
for someone far from home.
Let your face shine upon us, O God,
that we might be saved.

Renew the spirit of a world grown weary
with waiting and hoping.   *Mark 13:33*
Especially we pray for wars to end,
for hunger and poverty to be crowded out by abundance.
And we pray, too, for the church
because we also grow weary in our waiting and watching
for your power and glory to be made known.
Grant us clarity, passion, and true fellowship
so that we are awake to your presence.

Let your face shine upon the church
and all this weary world, we pray;
in the name of the One born in a manger
and coming again on clouds of glory. **Amen.**   *Mark 13:26*

INVITATION TO THE OFFERING
God has enriched us in every way—   *1 Cor. 1:5, 9*
in speech, knowledge, and spiritual gifts.
From the fellowship of Jesus Christ,
we are sent out
to share with thanksgiving what we have received.

PRAYER OF THANKSGIVING/DEDICATION
Faithful God,
we thank you that Christ is being revealed   *1 Cor. 1:5–8*
in every time and place
until he comes again in the fullness of glory.
Strengthen our testimony and spiritual gifts;

increase generosity in us, we pray,
as we wait for the day of our Lord Jesus Christ. **Amen.**

CHARGE

Beware.	*Mark 13:33,35, 37*
Keep alert.	
Keep awake.	
God is doing awesome things we do not expect.	*Isa. 64:3*
And Christ is coming near with great	
power and glory,	
and with tenderness.	*Mark 13:26, 28*

BLESSING

May God strengthen us to the end;	*1 Cor. 1:8*
Christ draw near to our very gates;	*Mark 13:29*
and the Holy Spirit awaken our spirits;	
until, with eager longing,	
we greet the day of our Lord Jesus Christ.	*Mark 13:26*

Question for Reflection

The weeks leading to Christmas are often filled with much activity. Along with work, school, and church responsibilities, there are special holiday festivities to which we will attend. Staying "awake," as Mark 13:24–37 stresses, may not be the problem—in fact, we may feel there are not enough hours in the day! Yet, this reading from Mark counsels us to be awake to, to pay attention to, what is most needful for our well-being and the well-being of the world: God's presence, God's appearing among us. Here at the beginning of Advent, how will you "keep alert" for God in the midst of so many responsibilities and distractions?

Household Prayer: Morning

Thank you, God, for the gift of life today.	
I give thanks that your face shines upon me—	*Ps. 80:3*
for you are my salvation.	
Lead me like a shepherd through this day.	*Ps. 80:1*
Strengthen me for whatever lies ahead.	
Grant me the spiritual gifts	
of peace, patience, kindness, and gentleness,	*Gal. 5:22–23*

for I want to show your love,
in word and deed, to others.
In Christ's name. Amen.

Household Prayer: Evening

Though you have told us to keep awake, O God,   *Mark 13:37*
you have also blessed us with rest and sleep.
Grant me such rest in the hours ahead
that I awaken with eager longing for a new day,
ready for you to be revealed
in mundane moments and ordinary encounters.
By your grace prepare me,
whether awake or asleep,
to greet you:
in the evening, or at midnight, or at cockcrow, or at dawn.   *Mark 13:35*
All times are in your hands,
and I, too, am in your hands, faithful God.   *Isa. 64:8*
In Jesus' name I rest and pray. Amen.

Second Sunday of Advent

Isaiah 40:1–11	2 Peter 3:8–15a
Psalm 85:1–2, 8–13	Mark 1:1–8

OPENING WORDS / CALL TO WORSHIP

A voice cries in the wilderness,   *Isa. 40:3–5*
"Prepare the way of the Lord; make God's way clear.
Lift up every valley; lower every mountain.
For the glory of the Lord shall be revealed."

CALL TO CONFESSION

God does not want anyone to perish,   *2 Pet. 3:9b*
but rather for all to come to repentance.
Therefore, let us confess our sins,
for God's salvation is at hand.   *Ps. 85:9*

PRAYER OF CONFESSION

**Faithful God, we confess that we have not led lives
of holiness.
We suffer from impatience, apathy, and greed;
we have not been at peace.
We repent of these offenses and turn to you in love.
Forgive our iniquity and pardon our sins,**   *Ps. 85:2*
**that we may walk in righteousness to the glory
of your name. Amen.**

DECLARATION OF FORGIVENESS

Brothers and sisters,
by the mercy of Christ, your sins are forgiven,
for salvation is at hand for all who turn to God.   *Ps. 85:2, 8-9*

PRAYER OF THE DAY

Loving God, you sent your prophet John
　to prepare your way among us,
to call us to repentance and make our
　pathways straight.　　　　　　　　　　　　*Mark 1:3–4*
Strengthen us to live lives of steadfast love
　and faithfulness
as we await the Messiah's return,
that all may see your reign of peace
through your just and gracious rule. **Amen.**

PRAYER FOR ILLUMINATION

Mighty God, send your Holy Spirit to speak peace,　　　*Ps. 85:8*
that the good news of this age may be proclaimed
through your word, which stands forever. **Amen.**　　　*Isa. 40:8*

PRAYERS OF INTERCESSION

As heralds of God's good tidings,　　　　　　　　　　*Isa. 40:9*
let us lift up our voices with strength this day
praying to the One who comforts, restores, and heals.

Let us pray for all leaders and people of the world.
You have created one human family to live in
　righteousness and peace.
Give us the wisdom to order our common life
according to your loving purposes,
that your glory may be revealed and all people shall
　see it together.　　　　　　　　　　　　　　　*Isa. 40:5*

Let us pray for your church.
You have given us the gift of the Messiah
so that your church may be steadfast and true.
Give us strength to follow your Son
until all have come to repentance and are reconciled
　by his love.

Let us pray for those who are sick, who suffer need,
　who are exiled or in danger.
You have made us for a holy purpose,
to comfort and care for each other.

Give us compassion to love our neighbor
and patience to care for those in need.

Let us pray for your creation.
Your faithfulness springs up from the ground,   *Ps. 85:11*
and your goodness looks down from the sky.
Rid us of the laziness and greed that diminish life
as you teach us to care for your creation together.

Let us remember those who have died.
Ever-living God,
one day in your presence is like a thousand years,
and a thousand years are like one day.   *2 Pet. 3:8*
Make us one with the saints,
who have found their eternal home in you,
Father, Son, and Holy Spirit. **Amen.**

INVITATION TO THE OFFERING
The Lord will give what is good,   *Ps. 85:12–13*
and our land will yield its increase.
May your righteousness go before God
and prepare a pathway for the Lord.
Let us offer our lives and labor to God
and fulfill our vows to the Most High.

PRAYER OF THANKSGIVING/DEDICATION
Lord, we give you thanks that in the coming of Christ
your steadfast love and faithfulness have met
and your righteousness and peace have kissed.   *Ps. 85:10*
May the gifts we offer this day lift up those in need
and prepare the way of your salvation. **Amen.**

CHARGE
The day of the Lord is coming;   *2 Pet. 3:13–14*
therefore strive to live in peace,
for God's salvation is near.

BLESSING
May faithfulness spring up from the ground   *Ps. 85:11–13*
and righteousness look down from heaven

as you walk in the way of peace,
and may the blessing of God,
Eternal Majesty, Living Word, and Holy Comforter,
be with you now and always.

Questions for Reflection

The prophet Isaiah announces good news: God comforts and strengthens
a wearied and exiled people in preparation for their homeward journey.
Mark's Gospel announces the good news of God in Jesus Christ: God
comes to turn the world right side up and baptize us with the Holy Spirit.
As we prepare to celebrate the birth of the Messiah, what is the beginning
of God's good news in your life, and how will it change the way you
approach this season of expectation and hope?

Household Prayer: Morning

Lord, how I love this season of new beginnings,
the opportunity to turn toward you and start again.
Empower me to be a messenger of good news,
and a leveling influence along the way,
as I seek to be one with you
in smoothing out the rough places I encounter. Amen.

Household Prayer: Evening

Lord, you have comforted me throughout this day
and rescued me from my exile.
Where I have flourished, I give you thanks;
where I have erred, I ask your forgiveness.
Protect me through the night
that I may rest in your realm of peace
where righteousness makes a home. Amen.

Third Sunday of Advent

Isaiah 61:1–4, 8–11   1 Thessalonians 5:16–24
Psalm 126 *or*   John 1:6–8, 19–28
Luke 1:46b–55

OPENING WORDS / CALL TO WORSHIP
The Promised One of God brings good news
    to the oppressed
and binds up the brokenhearted.   *Isa. 61:1*
We are witnesses to the light of Christ!   *John 1:7*
The Promised One of God proclaims liberty
    to captives
and release to prisoners.   *Isa. 61:1*
We are witnesses to the light of Christ!
The Promised One of God comforts all
    who mourn   *Isa. 61:2–3*
and gives a mantle of praise instead of a
    faint spirit.
Rejoicing always, praying without ceasing,   *1 Thess. 5:16–17, 21*
holding fast to what is good,
we are witnesses to the light of Christ!

CALL TO CONFESSION
Old habits and new wrongs wear ruts
through our lives and relationships.
[Water may be poured into the font.]

But God is able to restore us.   *Ps. 126:1, 4*
Like water coursing through a desert,
the waters of baptism flow through us,
reminding us that we belong to God
and are raised to new life.

PRAYER OF CONFESSION

Merciful God, you love justice;
why, then, do we persist in wrongdoing   *Isa. 61:8*
and every form of evil?   *1 Thess. 5:22*
You have given us the gift of your Spirit;
why, then, do we quench the Spirit among us?   *1 Thess. 5:19*
You have given us the words of the prophets   *1 Thess. 5:20*
and the Word himself;
why, then, do we despise and ignore
what we have heard from you?
You have sent the light into the world;   *John 3:19*
why, then, have we loved darkness rather than light?
Forgive us. Restore us.
Till and tend us as your garden   *Isa. 61:11*
until righteousness and praise spring up,
for the sake of Jesus Christ, in whose name we pray.
Amen.

DECLARATION OF FORGIVENESS

In Jesus Christ, the Lord has done great things for us!   *Ps. 126:3*
Even if we have gone out in tears,   *Ps. 126:6*
God brings us home shouting for joy.
Thanks be to God: we are forgiven!

PRAYER OF THE DAY

We thank you, O God,
for all those in Scripture who have pointed to Christ:
for your prophets Elijah and Isaiah, for other prophets,
   and for John.   *John 1:19–21*
We thank you, too,
for those in our lives who have pointed us to Christ:
pastors and teachers, strangers and friends.
Give us eyes to see him today
among those who are oppressed, imprisoned,   *Isa. 61:1–4*
brokenhearted, or beaten down,
and we will give our testimony, too:
how Christ releases and sets free;
how he turns ashes into garlands;
how he repairs and builds up what was ruined.
We, too, will point others to Jesus,
the Light of the world. **Amen.**

PRAYER FOR ILLUMINATION

Holy One,
giver of life and light,
as your word is read and proclaimed,
illumine our hearts and minds,
that by the power of the Holy Spirit,
our lives may reflect God's glory. **Amen.**

PRAYERS OF INTERCESSION

God who restores, *Ps. 126:1, 3*
you have done great things for us and we rejoice!
So often you have filled us with laughter, *Ps. 126:2*
even turning tears of sadness into shouts of joy. *Ps. 126:5–6*
You send prophets, who point the way to justice
and show the way to you.
We thank you for sending good news to us *Isa. 61:1–4*
and repairing so much that we have devastated.

In this season of light,
we lift up in prayer so many who wait in darkness:
people oppressed by poverty and discrimination,
by political upheaval or dangerous rulers;
people imprisoned wrongly
and also those imprisoned justly.
Right what is wrong among us and in us
and restore us to you,
to others,
to ourselves.
Make the brokenhearted whole again;
comfort those who mourn;
repair our ruined cities.
In all the jostling and jingling of these days,
do not let us lose sight of you
or those whom you especially came to serve:
people who are in need of healing,
people who are overlooked or underserved,
the ones who are lost,
and the ones we have made to feel little and least.

Light of the world,
live among us always,
full of grace and truth. **Amen.**

INVITATION TO THE OFFERING

At this time of year,
the abundance of some and the needs of so many
stand in marked contrast.
As we bring now our tithes and offerings,
may Christ's heart rejoice
and the needs of others be tended.

PRAYER OF THANKSGIVING/DEDICATION

Gracious God,
teach us to give thanks in all circumstances,   *1 Thess. 5:18*
for you are always with us.
Thank you for the privilege
of sharing what we have with others,
of giving ourselves away in love,
and of receiving the gifts that others share with us.
With our whole being,
spirit and soul and body,   *1 Thess. 5:23b*
we rejoice in you.
Through Jesus Christ our Lord. **Amen.**

CHARGE

Rejoice always.   *1 Thess. 5:16–17*
Pray without ceasing.
Witness to the light of Christ   *John 1:7*
so that all might believe through him.

BLESSING

Now may the God of peace   *1 Thess. 5:23*
call forth your complete dedication;
may the light of Christ shine upon you;
and the Holy Spirit fill you completely,
now and forever.

Question for Reflection

John 1:6–8, 19–28 reminds us that we are not the light, but with John we are called to testify as witnesses to the light, who is Jesus Christ. The verb "to bear witness" occurs thirty-three times in the Fourth Gospel! How can you bear witness, in this season of lights, to the true Light who has come into the world?

Household Prayer: Morning

Light of the world,
you greet me this morning with new possibilities.
Shine brightly, I pray,
until I see into the dark places of this world,
and into the dark places of my own life.
I want to follow you in paths of justice, *Isa. 61:8*
speak up with you for liberty, *Isa. 61:1*
and bend with you toward the brokenhearted,
even the broken places within myself.
I trade in my faint spirit for your mantle of praise— *Isa. 61:3, 10*
and with my whole being
I will rejoice in you. Amen.

Household Prayer: Evening

Restore me, O God, from the rush of the day.
Let me dream this night *Ps. 126:1–2*
of all the great things you have done.
As the darkness comes
and these little lights in my house glow,
I give thanks for the greater Light no darkness
    can overcome.
To anyone who mourns *Isa. 61:1–2*
or sits in prison
or fears danger this night,
bring the peace that only you can give. *John 14:27*
You are faithful, *1 Thess. 5:24*
and I know you will do this.
In Christ. Amen.

Fourth Sunday of Advent

2 Samuel 7:1–11, 16   Romans 16:25–27
Luke 1:46b–55   Luke 1:26–38
 or Psalm 89:1–4, 19–26

OPENING WORDS / CALL TO WORSHIP

My soul magnifies the Lord.   *Luke 1:46b*
My spirit rejoices in God my savior.
For the Mighty One has done great things,   *Luke 1:49*
and holy is God's name.

CALL TO CONFESSION

Let us confess our sins to the One
whose mercy endures from generation to generation.

PRAYER OF CONFESSION

Faithful God, we know that you are always there to guide us,
yet we often make plans without listening to you
and discover that our human agendas
can drown out our ability to hear your will for us.
We repent of these faults and turn to you in love.
Forgive our offenses and pardon our sins,
that our lives may magnify your holy name forever. Amen.

DECLARATION OF FORGIVENESS

Sisters and brothers,
by the faith of Christ, your sins are forgiven.
Blessed be the God of our salvation,
whose mercy is everlasting.

PRAYER OF THE DAY

Mighty God, your faithfulness is magnified in the coming of your Son,
in the long-awaited birth of the promised Messiah.

May we, like Mary, proclaim your greatness
as we rejoice in our Savior, Jesus Christ our Lord. **Amen.**

PRAYER FOR ILLUMINATION

Astonishing God, send your Holy Spirit upon us
as we await the coming of your Son.
Fill us with good things that we may conceive your reign on earth
and glorify you according to your Word;
through Jesus Christ our Savior. **Amen.**

PRAYERS OF INTERCESSION

Let us join our voices with Mary,
who celebrates God's greatness and sings of God's blessing
for all who are poor and oppressed.

Eternal God, we pray for the world,
that our warring ways may be overturned, even now,
through the birth, death, and resurrection of Christ;
for nothing is impossible with you.

We pray for the mission of your church,
that we may proclaim the good news of the age
as we rejoice in the gift of our Savior.

We pray for all who suffer,
that we may feed the hungry and lift up the lowly
through the power of your holy and life-giving Spirit.

We pray for your creation,
that we may safeguard its well-being
from generation to generation to your honor and glory.

We remember before you those who have died
and pray for those who will die today,
that they may rest with you eternally
in your kingdom where there is no end.

Through Christ, with Christ,
in the unity of the Holy Spirit,
we magnify you, almighty God,
forever and ever. **Amen.**

INVITATION TO THE OFFERING

Joining Mary's joyful song,
our souls proclaim the greatness of the Lord,
and our spirits rejoice in God our Savior.
With humble and grateful hearts,
let us bring our offerings to God.

PRAYER OF THANKSGIVING/DEDICATION

Holy God, your love is magnified in the gift of your Son,
whom you so freely share with us.
Bless these gifts that we offer
to lift up the lowly and fill the hungry   *Luke 1:52–53*
in your coming reign of justice and peace;
in Christ's name. **Amen.**

CHARGE

Do not be afraid, for God is with you   *Luke 1:28, 30*
and will strengthen you in your journey
through Jesus Christ, to whom be the glory forever!   *Rom. 16:27*

BLESSING

Magnify the Lord and rejoice,   *Luke 1:37, 46b*
for nothing is impossible with God.
And the blessing of God,
who creates, redeems, and restores,
be with you now and always.

Questions for Reflection

Mary's song proclaims that God is lifting up the lowly while scattering the proud, and feeding the hungry while sending the rich away with empty hands. How does this change the way you think about God's coming reign of justice and favor? How does this change the way you live?

Household Prayer: Morning

Expectant God,
Mary sings because she has new life in her,
the promise of your salvation.
Fill me with hope this day
as I lift my life to you and seek to do your will.
Look with favor on our world and all who are in need,
that your love may be magnified as I follow humbly in your way. Amen.

Household Prayer: Evening

Lord, as I come to you seeking rest this night,
I pray that all may find a home in you,
be disturbed by no one,
and be free of the afflictions of the evil one,
for you, O God, are mighty to save. Amen.

Nativity of the Lord/
Proper I / Christmas Eve

Isaiah 9:2–7   Titus 2:11–14
Psalm 96   Luke 2:1–14 (15–20)

OPENING WORDS / CALL TO WORSHIP
With the prophet Isaiah,   *Isa. 9:2–7*
we proclaim the promise of God:
The people who walked in darkness
have seen a great light;
those who lived in a land of deep darkness—
on them light has shined.
For a child has been born for us,
a son given to us;
authority rests upon his shoulders;
and he is named
Wonderful Counselor, Mighty God,
Everlasting Father, Prince of Peace.
[or]
Good news of great joy!
People who walked in darkness now live in
    great light.   *Isa. 9:2*
Good news of great joy!
Oppression and war will not have the last word.   *Isa. 9:4–5*
Good news of great joy!   *Luke 2:10–11, 14*
A Savior is born, who is the Messiah, the Lord.
Glory to God in the highest, and on earth, peace.
[or]
Because Christ has been born in the world,
people who walked in darkness now live in great light.   *Isa. 9:2*
Because Christ has been born in the world,
the power to oppress and kill will not stand.   *Isa. 9:4–5*

20

Because Christ has been born in the world,
we respond in wonder:

with the angels, we sing glory to God; *Luke 2:14*
with the shepherds, we share the good news; *Luke 2:15–18*
with Mary, we ponder the words of this night, *Luke 2:19*
and the Word that has come into the world:
Immanuel.

CALL TO CONFESSION

Friends, the grace of Christ educates us *Titus 2:12*
so that we can live sensible, ethical, and godly lives.
On this eve of his birth,
we confess that we struggle to receive him still.

PRAYER OF CONFESSION

God of Love Incarnate,
we confess that, with the shepherds, *Luke 2:9*
we are terrified of your glory;
for in glory's light we see plainly
all that is wrong in the world:
how oppression still enslaves; *Isa. 9:4*
how garments of war are still stained with blood; *Isa. 9:5*
how those seeking refuge still find no place of safety. *Luke 2:7*
We also see what is wrong in us:
how passionately we pursue the things of this world,
but forget to ponder the mystery of faith;
how we do not practice the peace you intend
in our relationships, our community,
or even in the church.
Forgive us, we pray,
and help us not to be afraid.
Like the shepherds,
we want to follow and find you.
In the Savior's name we pray. Amen.

DECLARATION OF FORGIVENESS

Good news! *Luke 2:10*
Great joy!
In Jesus Christ
the grace of God has appeared, *Titus 2:11*
bringing salvation to all.

Glory to God in heaven,   *Luke 2:14*
and on earth, peace.

PRAYER OF THE DAY
Glorious God,
on this Christmas Eve,
we sing beloved carols of Bethlehem,
of shepherds and angels,
of Mary and Joseph,
and the infant Jesus, our Savior.
Is there yet a new song we can sing to you?   *Ps. 96:1*
A song to be learned from the heavens and the earth: *Ps. 96:11–13a*
where the roar of the sea,
the exultation of the fields,
and the joy of the trees
are already raised in a chorus of glad rejoicing,
ready to welcome you.
Even if no ear may hear your coming,
help us hear the music of creation.
Then, with the whole cosmos,
we will sing of your salvation,   *Ps. 96:2–3*
declare your glory,
and in a crescendo of praise, bless your name:
Wonderful Counselor, Mighty God, Everlasting Father,
    Prince of Peace! **Amen.**   *Isa. 9:6b*

PRAYER FOR ILLUMINATION
We would make room for you this night of all nights,
    dear Lord:
room in our minds and hearts;
room also in our life together.
Let your word be born in us anew
so that, by the power of the Holy Spirit,
your splendor shines in us and through us.
In Jesus' name we pray. **Amen.**

PRAYERS OF INTERCESSION
Glory to you, O God,
for good news of great joy that you give to all people.
Thank you for Jesus Christ, the Messiah,

who lived among us and now reigns on high.
Thank you for his light that shines in the darkness.
With the angels, we sing praise to you,
celebrating your glory in all the earth,
in the Son given to us,
and in your promised salvation.

Gathered as a community on this Christmas Eve,
we pray for your church in every place,
that we may make known to others   *Luke 2:17*
what has been told to us about this child.
Help us to bear Christ's light in every place of need.
Draw near to those who spend this night apart from community:
travelers and those far from home,
people who live alone,
one who waits in a hospital room,
one who sits in a prison cell,
one who is working deep in the night,
one estranged from family or friends.
Comfort those who are poor and vulnerable:
the child at risk, the homeless on the streets,
the family that is hungry,
and those contending with prejudice and scorn.

Restore those who have lost faith, lost hope,
or simply lost their way.
End the hostilities and wars we construct
by ushering in the endless peace of your design.
Establish your reign of justice and righteousness.   *Isa. 9:7*
You are the Lord of hosts who, with zeal, will do this;
through Jesus Christ our Savior. **Amen.**

INVITATION TO THE OFFERING
Because God so loved the world,   *John 3:16*
God sent the Son into the world.
In response to this good news of great joy,
we offer songs of praise,
tithes and offerings,
and acts of service.

PRAYER OF THANKSGIVING/DEDICATION

Great God, accept these gifts we offer   *Titus 2:13*
as we wait in hope for your coming again.
Use all that we have and all that we are
as you bring light in every darkness,   *Isa. 9:2, 4, 5, 7*
ease heavy burdens,
and turn our endless warring
into your endless peace.
In Christ's name, we ask it. **Amen.**

CHARGE

Go out this night in joy and hope,
with the song of the angels on your lips to tell:
Glory to God in the highest, and on earth, peace.   *Luke 2:14*
[or]
Do not be afraid—
the light still shines in the darkness,   *John 1:5*
and the darkness cannot overcome it.
Bear the light of Christ into the world
with hope and great joy!

BLESSING

May the love of God enfold us,
the joy of Christ encompass us,
and the Holy Spirit encourage us,
as we wait in hope for Christ to come again.
[or]
The love of God,
the light of Christ,
and the joy of the Holy Spirit
abide with you this holy night
and forever.

Questions for Reflection

In Isaiah's prophecy in chapter 9 and the birth narrative in Luke 2, the glory of God is described as a light shining in the darkness. On this eve of Christmas, where is there a deep need for God's light to shine with love, with hope, or with peace in your life; in the life of someone you love; or in a troubled part of the world? What is your prayer for light in this darkness?

Household Prayer: Morning

God of hope, peace, joy, and love,
this day is so full!
For children, this day is one of excitement and anticipation;
for others, this day is filled with responsibilities and activity.
Some are traveling this day to be with family or friends,
while others spend the day quietly and alone.
Be with us in all our varied circumstances and moods.
I pray that I, and all those within my circles of care,
will be especially attentive to the angels' good news:
that you have come to dwell among us in Jesus Christ,
full of grace and truth.
In this is our great joy. Amen.

Household Prayer: Evening

Loving God,
this night holds so much for me—
people and places from long ago
are brought near in memories redeemed;
my present companions,
as well as present cares,
are held in tenderness.
Lord, I would hold the whole world in my hands,
turning it round and round,
so that your light would shine everywhere on everyone
with hope and peace.
As it is, I utter this prayer instead—
my little light in the shades of night:
Hold those I love and all the world
in your sure and tender hands,
as a mother holds her newborn child.
Let your face shine upon us with peace.
Gather up the past, the present, and the future
into your eternity,
where all is reconciled and you are all in all.
In the name of him who was born this night,
Jesus, who is Christ the Lord. Amen.

Nativity of the Lord/
Proper III / Christmas Day

Isaiah 52:7–10   Hebrews 1:1–4 (5–12)
Psalm 98   John 1:1–14

OPENING WORDS / CALL TO WORSHIP
And the Word became flesh and lived among us,   *John 1:14*
and we have seen his glory, full of grace and truth.

CALL TO CONFESSION
Let us confess our sins with boldness,
for God's light has come to shine in our darkness
and remove the shadow of our sins.

PRAYER OF CONFESSION
Faithful God, you love righteousness and hate wickedness,   *Heb. 1:9*
yet we have not lived lives of integrity and truth;
we have failed to honor you.
We repent of these faults and turn to you in love.
Pardon our offenses and purify our hearts,
that our lives may glorify you to the ends of the earth,
for the sake of our Savior, Jesus Christ. Amen.

DECLARATION OF FORGIVENESS
Sisters and brothers, receive the good news:
the light of Christ shines in our darkness,
to bring light and life to all.
By the gift of Christ, your sins are forgiven.
Praise God for our victory in Christ.

PRAYER OF THE DAY
Wondrous God, we praise you and bless you
for the gift of your only begotten Son,

the true light who enlightens everyone
that has come into the world.
May all who receive him and believe in his name
be born anew as beloved children of your redeeming purpose.
In Christ's name we pray. **Amen.**

PRAYER FOR ILLUMINATION

Loving God, before time and space
your living Word was with you creating all things.
In the fullness of time, he came to bring peace
and to show us how to love.
By the anointing of your Holy Spirit,
inspire us to share his light wherever we go
as we carry your good news of salvation
to the ends of the earth. **Amen.**

PRAYERS OF INTERCESSION

[Optional response to each intercession:
Light of the world, shine in our lives.]

Eternal God, in the midst of strife and warfare,
may your peace may be known throughout the world.

As your church announces the good news of salvation,
may we share the gift of Christ in prayer and action.

In sickness, suffering, and need,
may your healing love dispel all darkness.

As all creation shouts with joy,
may we care for earth, sea, and sky in reverence of you.

In all of our beginnings and in our endings,
may we be one with you eternally.

Through Christ, with Christ,
in the unity of the Holy Spirit,
we praise you, almighty God,
now and forever. **Amen.**

INVITATION TO THE OFFERING

With grateful hearts for the gift of our Savior,
let us bring our gifts to God.

PRAYER OF THANKSGIVING/DEDICATION

O Majesty on high,
whom angels worship
in thanksgiving for your Son,
bless these gifts we offer
that they may bring light
to the darkened corners of our world;
in Christ's name we pray. **Amen.**

CHARGE

Go in peace to bring comfort and healing
and to announce good news in the name of Christ.

BLESSING

The blessing of God, the One who creates,
redeems, and sustains us eternally,
be with you now and always.

Question for Reflection

Christmas Day brings the astonishing news that God is revealed to us in
Jesus Christ. Jesus is the imprint of God's being and the reflection of God's
glory (Heb. 1:3), and we, in turn, are God's offspring though Christ (John
1:12). How does this news shape your self-awareness and change the way
you live?

Household Prayer: Morning

Eternal God, as I celebrate the birthday of Jesus,
may I sing of your love all the days of my life,
for you have made me your child forever.
In Christ I pray. Amen.

Household Prayer: Evening

Lord, I give thanks for the blessings of this day (which I now name),
and I ask your forgiveness for the places
where I have failed to reveal your love (which I now name).
I give thanks that you have become one of us,
that I may become more like you.
As I sleep this night,
may your goodness shape me to more lovingly reflect
your light in the world. Amen.

First Sunday after Christmas

Isaiah 61:10–62:3　　　　Galatians 4:4–7
Psalm 148　　　　　　　Luke 2:22–40

OPENING WORDS / CALL TO WORSHIP

Praise the Lord!
Praise God from the heavens.　　　　　　　　　　*Ps. 148:1*
Young men and women alike,
old and young together!　　　　　　　　　　　*Ps. 148:12*
Let us praise the name of the Lord,
whose name alone is exalted above earth and heaven.　*Ps. 148:13*
Alleluia!

CALL TO CONFESSION

Jesus our Lord came into an indifferent world,
yet his life revealed the inner thoughts of many.　　*Luke 2:34-35*
Let us confess our sins before God and one another
that we may receive release from our sin.

PRAYER OF CONFESSION

Merciful God,
we confess that we have not lived as your
faithful children.
We have kept silent in midst of prejudice
and hatred.
We have been idle in the face of violence
and injustice.
We have not been a light to the nations,
and our lives have not revealed your glory.　　*Isa. 62:1-2*
Forgive us, Merciful God.
Repair the ugliness of our sin
and restore in us your beautiful grace;　　　　*Isa. 62:3*
through Jesus Christ our Lord. Amen.

DECLARATION OF FORGIVENESS

Beloved of God,
as a bridegroom decks himself with a garland,
as a bride adorns herself with her jewels,
God covers us with the robe of righteousness.   *Isa. 61:10*
Know that you are forgiven in Jesus Christ
and live as God's beloved.

PRAYER OF THE DAY

Saving God, the prophet Anna and righteous Simeon
   sang your praise   *Luke 2:25–38*
and proclaimed Jesus our Lord
to all who were looking for the redemption
   of Jerusalem.
Let us who seek redemption in this day prepare
   our hearts,
that we may believe the good news of Jesus,
receive the light of salvation,
and live according to your word.
In Jesus' name we pray. **Amen.**

PRAYER FOR ILLUMINATION

As you led Simeon to embrace the infant Jesus,   *Luke 2:27*
guide us, Holy Spirit, by your gracious light
that we may welcome your saving Word. **Amen.**

PRAYERS OF INTERCESSION

As children of God and heirs of the promise,   *Gal. 4:6–7*
let us pray to the Lord, saying,
Loving God, hear our prayer.

For the holy church of God,
that all who have been baptized into Christ
may shine like the dawn,   *Isa. 62:1*
bear witness to the Good News of Jesus,
and light the way of salvation in Jesus' name,
   let us pray to the Lord: Loving God, **hear our prayer.**

For the nations of the earth,
that governments and those in authority may protect
   the vulnerable,

shelter the oppressed,
and pursue the way of peace,
let us pray to the Lord: Loving God, **hear our prayer.**

For our city *[town]* and for all places of human interaction
    and livelihood,
that kindness may abound,
compassion prevail,
and harmony endure,
let us pray to the Lord: Loving God, **hear our prayer.**

For the planet earth, our home,
that we may honor her gifts,
respect her limitations,
and protect her resources,
let us pray to the Lord: Loving God, **hear our prayer.**

For those troubled with illness, hardship, or conflict,
that they may receive healing for their bodies,
release from their burdens,
and mending of their brokenness,
let us pray to the Lord: Loving God, **hear our prayer.**

Hear us, O God, for our eyes have seen your salvation.   *Luke 2:30*
Let your light shine through us and fill the world
with the radiance of your love revealed in Jesus Christ,
    our Lord,
who with you and the Holy Spirit reigns in glory. **Amen.**

INVITATION TO THE OFFERING

As the earth brings forth its shoots   *Isa. 61:11*
and as a garden causes what is sown in it to spring up,
so will God cause righteousness and praise to spring up
    before all the nations.
With thankful hearts, let us offer ourselves and our
    gifts to God.

PRAYER OF THANKSGIVING/DEDICATION

Loving God,
we give you thanks for the light of the world, Jesus Christ,
through whom we have received adoption as your children.   *Gal. 4:5*
With Jesus our brother,
we dedicate ourselves in ministry to the world,
that we may live as heirs of your promises   *Gal. 4:7*
to the honor and glory of your name. **Amen.**

CHARGE

Go forth into the world rejoicing.
Spread the good news of Christ
our light and our redeemer.

BLESSING

May God, redeemer of Israel, dismiss us in peace;
may Jesus Christ, Son of God, Son of Mary, uphold us in love;
may the Holy Spirit, the power of God, guide us in truth.

Question for Reflection

Consider what it means to be a child of God by adoption. What does it mean to you to think of yourself as a brother or sister of Jesus, who is the Son of God?

Household Prayer: Morning

In you, O God, I will greatly rejoice:
in speaking, I will greatly rejoice;
in silence, I will greatly rejoice;
in travels, I will greatly rejoice;
in resting, I will greatly rejoice;
in working, I will greatly rejoice;
in leisure, I will greatly rejoice;
in duties, I will greatly rejoice;
in freedom, I will greatly rejoice.
O God, my whole being exults in you,
and my life shall evermore declare your praise,
my light, my love, my joy. Amen.

Lord, let your servant sleep in peace this night
and fulfill your gracious word.
Reveal to me the salvation that you have prepared
for all people.
With Jesus Christ, help me be a light to the nations
and a sign of your glorious promise to Israel. Amen.

Second Sunday after Christmas

Jeremiah 31:7–14 *or* Sirach 24:1–12
Psalm 147:12–20 *or*
   Wisdom of Solomon 10:15–21

Ephesians 1:3–14
John 1:(1–9) 10–18

OPENING WORDS / CALL TO WORSHIP

Sing praise to God, who gathers us here;   *Jer. 31:7–14*
from the ends of the earth we come.
With a word of promise, a spring of water,
   a loaf of bread, and a cup of wine,
     God turns our mourning into dancing,
our sorrow into joy.

CALL TO CONFESSION

[Pouring water into the font]
The gift of God's grace is lavished upon us—   *Eph. 1:3–8*
poured out like water—
   through the life and death of the risen Lord.

Trusting in the love and goodness of God,
   let us confess our sin.

PRAYER OF CONFESSION

Holy God, you have given us everything;   *John 1:1–18*
we have failed to respond with gratitude.
In Jesus Christ, you have given us your Word;
we answer with empty promises and lies.
In Jesus Christ, you have given us your light;
we try to hide ourselves from your glory.
In Jesus Christ, you have given us your life;
even this precious gift we have not received.
Have mercy on us, O God; forgive us.

In Jesus Christ, give us the faith and power
to become what you created us to be:
beloved children, full of grace and truth. Amen.

DECLARATION OF FORGIVENESS
[Lifting water from the font]
This is God's promise,   *Eph. 1:11–14*
the sign and seal of your redemption:
You have been called by God,
claimed in Christ,
set free through the Spirit.

Believe this good news:
In Jesus Christ you are forgiven.
Thanks be to God.

PRAYER OF THE DAY
God of every blessing, we rejoice   *Eph. 1:3–6, 9–12*
that you have chosen us from long ago,
adopted us as your beloved children,
and gathered us into your presence.
Now make known in our hearts and lives
your eternal purpose for heaven and earth
so that we may live, this day and always,
for the glory of Christ our Lord. **Amen.**

PRAYER FOR ILLUMINATION
Shine upon us, God of glory,   *John 1:5, 14*
and by your Spirit reveal to us
the grace and truth of Jesus Christ,
your Word made flesh. **Amen.**

PRAYERS OF INTERCESSION
[A time of silence may be kept after each ellipsis.]
Let us pray to the Lord, saying,
To you, O Lord, we pray: come and save your people.

Hope of the prophets, joy of the people,   *Jer. 31:7–14*
source of all life and song of salvation,
to you, O Lord, we pray:
come and save your people.

Remember those who are lost and scattered,
wandering without direction or hope. . . .
Gather them up into your flock and fold;
put a new song of praise upon their lips.
To you, O Lord, we pray:
come and save your people.

Remember those who are hungry and thirsty,
languishing because of what they lack. . . .
Satisfy their needs through your abundant love;
lead them to springs of water that never fail.
To you, O Lord, we pray:
come and save your people.

Remember those who are sick and suffering,
held in the grip of illness and pain. . . .
Set them free from their affliction;
heal them and renew their strength.
To you, O Lord, we pray:
come and save your people.

Remember those who are sad and grieving,
unable to laugh, to dance, to sing. . . .
Give them the peace that can never perish
and the joy that can never be taken away.
To you, O Lord, we pray:
come and save your people.

Come and save your people, O Lord,
so that we may rejoice in your goodness
and be radiant in your presence,
singing songs of thanks and praise
to the glory of your holy name. **Amen.**

INVITATION TO THE OFFERING
Let us gather up the gifts of the Lord,   *Ps. 147:14*
who fills us with finest wheat.
With thanksgiving, let us offer our lives
to God, the giver of life.

PRAYER OF THANKSGIVING/DEDICATION

We give you thanks, God of all creation,   *Ps. 147:12–20*
for the power of your life-giving Word,
making the winds blow and the waters flow.
Receive these gifts from our hands,
and use them to bring peace and blessing
to all your children; in Jesus' name. **Amen.**

CHARGE

Let your life bear witness to Christ,   *John 1:7–9*
the light who has come to the world. **Amen.**

BLESSING

Children of God—chosen, beloved—   *Eph. 1:3–6*
in Christ every blessing is yours. **Alleluia!**

Questions for Reflection

The theme of "fullness" runs through all the lectionary readings for this day. God satisfies the people with bounty (Jer. 31:14) and fills them with finest wheat (Ps. 147:14). Jesus, God's Word made flesh, reveals the fullness of God's grace and truth (John 1:14), a fullness from which we all receive grace upon grace (John 1:16). The apostle says that in the fullness of time (Eph. 1:10; cf. Gal. 4:4) all things will be gathered into God. Where is there fullness in your life? Where is there emptiness? How have you experienced the fullness of God's grace?

Household Prayer: Morning

At the beginning of this day, O God,
you are with me, like light scattering darkness.
Be with me to the end—
and to the beginning of the life
that even death cannot destroy;
through Jesus Christ the Lord. Amen.

Household Prayer: Evening

God of all glory, I give you thanks
for the fullness of this day
and the grace upon grace you have given me.
Now hold me close to your heart
and let me rest in the grace of Christ,
the light of the world. Amen.

Epiphany of the Lord

Isaiah 60:1–6   Ephesians 3:1–12
Psalm 72:1–7, 10–14   Matthew 2:1–12

OPENING WORDS / CALL TO WORSHIP
Arise, shine; for your light has come.   *Isa. 60:1*
Behold the glory of the Lord. Alleluia!

CALL TO CONFESSION
Isaiah proclaimed: Darkness shall cover the earth,   *Isa. 60:2*
and thick darkness the peoples;
but the Lord will arise upon you,
and God's glory will appear over you.
Let us acknowledge the darkness in our lives,
repent of our sin,
and receive the light of God's mercy.

PRAYER OF CONFESSION
Merciful God, Light of the world,
we confess that we have not resisted the darkness
of sin.   *Isa. 60:2*
You deliver the poor and the helpless,   *Ps. 72:12–14*
but we have ignored their cry.
You take pity on the weak and the destitute,
but our hearts are hard in the face of their need.
You heal the wounded and save the oppressed
but we have placed our trust in the callous violence
of war.
Forgive us, we pray.
Awaken in us sincere repentance
that we may shine with the light of your saving grace;   *Isa. 60:5*
through Jesus Christ our Lord. Amen.

DECLARATION OF FORGIVENESS

Beloved of God,
thrill and rejoice in God's goodness. *Isa. 60:5*
In the name of Jesus Christ, you are forgiven.

PRAYER OF THE DAY

God of every nation,
by the light of a wondrous star
you led wandering magi to the humble infant Jesus,
revealing to them your salvation for the world.
In the miraculous and the mundane,
in union with all who have glimpsed the light of your grace,
lead us to Christ,
that we may offer our worship
and serve him with sincerity of heart;
for he lives with you and the Holy Spirit,
one God, forever. **Amen.**

PRAYER FOR ILLUMINATION

O God, nations shall come to your light *Isa. 60:3*
and rulers to the brightness of your dawn.
By the compelling radiance of your Spirit,
draw us near, reveal your truth,
and teach us faithful obedience to your holy Word. **Amen.**

PRAYERS OF INTERCESSION

With the boldness and confidence of God's children,
    let us pray, saying, *Eph. 3:12*
Gracious God, Lord of Light, hear our prayer.

Loving God, in Christ you embrace people of
    every nation
and make them members of the same body, *Eph. 3:6*
sharers in the promise of the gospel.
For the holy church of God,
that through its faithful witness
the wisdom of God in its rich variety *Eph. 3:10*
be known in heaven and earth,
Gracious God, Lord of Light, **hear our prayer.**

Loving God,
you judge the people with righteousness and the poor
    with justice. *Ps. 72:2*
For nations, rulers, and authorities
to forsake violence and be guided by the light of truth,
that righteousness may flourish and justice abound
    in every land, *Ps. 72:7*
Gracious God, Lord of Light, **hear our prayer.**

Loving God,
wise men from afar came to visit the holy family
and found a place of rest and worship.
For our city *[town]* and for all who live here,
that we may be a community of hospitality,
welcoming the stranger
and sheltering the refugee,
Gracious God, Lord of Light, **hear our prayer.**

Loving God,
in your providence, the land yields prosperity
    for the people *Ps. 72:3*
that righteousness may prevail in the land.
For our planet earth,
that we may dwell peacefully with nature,
be good stewards of its resources,
and share its abundance for the sake of
    human flourishing,
Gracious God, Lord of Light, **hear our prayer.**

Loving God,
you defend the cause of the poor, *Ps. 72:4*
give deliverance to the needy,
and save those who are oppressed.
For those who suffer the cruelty of poverty,
and all who endeavor to transform systems of
    economic injustice,
Gracious God, Lord of Light, **hear our prayer.**

Loving God,
you take pity on the weak. *Ps. 72:13*
For those whose bodies are enfeebled by disease
or whose spirits are debilitated by illness,
that they may be restored to wholeness of life,
Gracious God, Lord of Light, **hear our prayer.**

Loving God,
your servant Paul was imprisoned
for preaching the good news of Jesus. *Eph. 3:1*
For any who are wrongly incarcerated
that they may be liberated,
and for those whose guilt is valid and imprisonment
warranted
that they may know genuine repentance of their sin
and reconciliation with their community,
Gracious God, Lord of Light, **hear our prayer.**

Gracious God,
because you have called us your children,
we are bold to ask for what we need,
confident in your goodness *Eph. 3:12*
through faith in our Lord and brother, Jesus Christ.
Amen.

INVITATION TO THE OFFERING
The magi brought gifts to Christ at his nativity
and offered their lives in worship.
With thankful hearts, let us offer ourselves and our gifts to God.

PRAYER OF THANKSGIVING/DEDICATION
Loving God,
we give you thanks for the light of the world, Jesus Christ,
through whom we have become fellow heirs, *Eph. 3:6*
members of the same body, and sharers in your promise.
Receive the gifts we offer
in union with Jesus our brother,
and help us to live to the honor and glory of your name. **Amen.**

CHARGE

Go forth into the world.
Proclaim the good news of Christ.
Receive the inheritance of God's promise.
Live in the light of the gospel.

BLESSING

God, ruler of heaven and earth, dismiss you in peace;
Jesus Christ, light of the world, uphold you in love;
the Holy Spirit, revealer of God's mystery, lead you in truth.

Question for Reflection

Warned in a dream of Herod's evil intentions, the magi "left for their own country by another road." What could it mean for you to take "another road" as the church concludes the celebrations of the Christmas season?

Household Prayer: Morning

Loving God,
do not let my good intentions become a means of evil.
Do not let my trust become cooperation with sin.
Do not let my naiveté become an opportunity for wickedness.
Make me prudent in acts of mercy,
firm in my resistance to evil,
and wise in my discernment of wrong,
for the sake of Jesus Christ. Amen.

Household Prayer: Evening

Loving God,
in the journey of life
guide me by the star that leads to Jesus,
that I may return to you transformed by his love. Amen.

Baptism of the Lord /
First Sunday after the Epiphany

Genesis 1:1–5	Acts 19:1–7
Psalm 29	Mark 1:4–11

OPENING WORDS / CALL TO WORSHIP

In the beginning,   *Gen. 1:1–2; Mark 1:1, 9–11*
God created the heavens and the earth.
The Spirit of God
swept over the face of the waters;
then God said: Let there be light,
and God saw that it was good.
At the beginning of his ministry,
Jesus was baptized by John.
The heavens opened,
and the Spirit descended like a dove;
then God said: This is my beloved Son,
in whom I am well pleased.

CALL TO CONFESSION

[Pouring water into the font]
A prophet appeared in the wilderness,   *Acts 19:4; Mark 1:2–5*
calling the people to repent, be baptized,
and prepare the way of the Lord.
We return to the water to confess our sins,
giving thanks for the grace of Jesus Christ,
the one who has come to save us.

PRAYER OF CONFESSION

God of all glory, you look from heaven   *Ps. 29:1; Mark 1:7*
and see us as we are—
not worthy to kneel at your feet,
not ready to welcome your way.

Forgive us, gracious God.
In Christ, stoop down to save us;
loosen the ties that bind us to sin
and set us free to love and serve you;
in Jesus' name. Amen.

DECLARATION OF FORGIVENESS

[Lifting water from the font]
Hear the good news of the gospel: *Mark 1:11*
As a voice from heaven said to Jesus,
so God says to each of us:
You are my beloved child,
and with you I am well pleased.
In Jesus Christ we are forgiven.
Thanks be to God.

PRAYER OF THE DAY

God of heaven and earth,   *Gen. 1:1; Ps. 29:9;*
we gather in the name of Jesus   *Acts 19:5–7; Mark 1:8*
to hear your holy Word
and to be immersed in your Spirit.
Speak to us with grace and truth
and pour out your love upon us
so that this temple may resound
with joyful shouts of glory;
through Christ our Lord. **Amen.**

PRAYER FOR ILLUMINATION

Send down your Holy Spirit, O God—   *Mark 1:10–11*
tear open the veil of heaven
and speak to us as beloved children
so that we may hear and believe
the good news of your Word made flesh,
Jesus Christ our Lord. **Amen.**

PRAYERS OF INTERCESSION

Let us pray to the Lord, saying,
Give strength, O Lord, and bless us with peace.

All-glorious God, *Ps. 29:11*
maker of heaven and earth,
hear us as we pray:
Give strength, O Lord,
and bless us with peace.

We pray for the world you have made. . . .
Move again over these troubled waters,
steeped in chemicals and stained with blood.
Where carelessness and violence bring chaos
restore order, goodness, and life.
Give strength, O Lord,
and bless us with peace.

We pray for the church you have redeemed. . . .
Renew in us the gifts of your Spirit
and the call to Christian discipleship.
Where history and heresy have divided us,
make us one in the baptism we share.
Give strength, O Lord,
and bless us with peace.

We pray for the peoples you have created. . . .
Give to the leaders of all nations
the wisdom to know what is good.
Where people are poor and hungry
provide justice and daily bread.
Give strength, O Lord,
and bless us with peace.

We pray for the loved ones you have given us. . . .
Bless our families, friends, and neighbors;
keep them safe from trouble and danger.
Where there is sorrow, sickness, or suffering
send your Spirit of comfort and healing.
Give strength, O Lord,
and bless us with peace.

All this we pray in the name of the Lord Jesus, *Acts 19:5*
whose voice is our strength and salvation,
whose breath is the Spirit of peace. **Amen.**

INVITATION TO THE OFFERING

The earth belongs to God, our creator;   *Gen. 1:1, 4; Ps. 29:2*
every good thing is a gift from the Lord.
Let us glorify God through the gifts of our lives.

PRAYER OF THANKSGIVING/DEDICATION

We give you thanks, O God,   *Acts 19:1–7;*
for every blessing and spiritual gift   *Mark 1:4–11*
you have poured out upon us.
Let the gifts of our lives
be a source of blessing in your world,
all to the glory of your holy name. **Amen.**

CHARGE

Go forth in the light and love of God,   *Gen. 1:3; Ps. 29:2*
giving glory to God in all that you do.

BLESSING

Beloved children of God   *Mark 1:10–11*
(Spirit, Son, and Father),
all the blessings of heaven are yours. Alleluia!

Questions for Reflection

What is the difference between baptism with water alone (John's baptism; see Acts 19:3, Mark 1:8) and baptism with the Holy Spirit (baptism into Jesus; see Acts 19:4–5, Mark 1:8)? Why is it still important to use water in baptism? What does water mean in your daily life? What difference does the Holy Spirit make in baptism? What difference does the Holy Spirit make in your daily life?

Household Prayer: Morning

Living God, maker of light,
thank you for the gift of this day.
Let me be a light in your world
so that people will look at me
and see the goodness of your creation;
in Jesus' name I pray. Amen.

Living God, maker of light,
thank you for the gift of this night.
Let me be at peace in your presence
so that I may rest, be restored,
and arise to praise your glory;
in Jesus' name I pray. Amen.

Second Sunday after the Epiphany

1 Samuel 3:1–10 (11–20)   1 Corinthians 6:12–20
Psalm 139:1–6, 13–18   John 1:43–51

OPENING WORDS / CALL TO WORSHIP
The one who calls you together this day
yearns for each of you and for all people to hear
   and be blessed.
Speak, Lord, for your servants are listening.   *1 Sam. 3:9*
Blessed is the One who comes bringing
   trustworthy words
for the healing of the world.
Speak, Lord, for your servants are listening.

CALL TO CONFESSION
Assured that the One who calls us to hear and obey
already knows the confessions of our hearts
and is ready to forgive,
let us confess our sin before God and before one another.

PRAYER OF CONFESSION
Holy God, you see into each of us
and know us fully
as creatures in need of your constant care.
We confess that we have neither heard your word
nor followed your will.
We have failed our nation, neighbors, families, friends,
**   and ourselves.**
Give us ears to hear your wisdom.
Lead us to honesty and faith
so that we may begin again with renewed strength;
in Jesus' name. Amen.

DECLARATION OF FORGIVENESS

God knows the hearts of those who seek forgiveness,
and by grace you have been saved.
In Jesus' name you are forgiven.
Your sins are no more.
You have been made clean.
God strengthens you with freedom
through the Holy Spirit, in Christ Jesus.

PRAYER OF THE DAY

You invite us, O God, to live in your ways,
and you give us to each other to know and to love
as we journey in this life.
Show us your will for all creation.
Help us to listen to your urgings with prayerful hearts
so that we may honor what you have made,
in the name of the holy Trinity, one God, now and forever. **Amen.**

PRAYER FOR ILLUMINATION

By your Holy Spirit, O God, open our ears, our eyes,
our hearts, and our minds to the Holy Word
so that it comes to rule within us for Jesus' sake. **Amen.**

PRAYERS OF INTERCESSION

Let us pray for all the earth, the church, and all those in need, saying,
God of grace, hear our prayer.

Let us pray for the world:
for leaders of nations,
that wisdom and integrity will prevail for the good of all people,
especially the poor;
for regions torn by conflict, that peace may reign
and living become an enterprise of construction rather than
    destruction;
God of grace, **hear our prayer.**

Let us pray for all people of faith:
for the unity of the body of Christ,
that divisions might not turn people away from the church;
for Hindus, Muslims, Buddhists, and Jews,

that wherever prayers are raised up, the one God of all will hear;
for all people who nurture life in the name of a greater good;
God of grace, **hear our prayer.**

Let us pray for our own nation:
for the president and Congress, the Supreme Court and all judges,
for state governments, city councils, school boards,
and all who have power to make policy,
that all consideration be given
to what is most healthy for people and creatures;
God of grace, **hear our prayer.**

Let us pray for those in need:
for all who are hungry in our nation and world,
for those who have no home and no employment,
for those who are either unjustly or justly imprisoned,
for parents and children who live in fear for any reason,
and for all who are in mourning;
God of grace, **hear our prayer.**

For all other concerns of this assembly now spoken aloud or silently, . . .
[A time of silence is kept.]
God of grace, **hear our prayer.**

With thanksgiving,
we remember all those who have shaped us in your ways, O God.
Receive our prayers and grant whatever you see
that your people need;
through Jesus Christ, our Lord. **Amen.**

INVITATION TO THE OFFERING

Jesus promised that you and I will come to see
heaven opened and angels dancing in splendor.   *John 1:51*
Our offerings are a thanksgiving for these gifts.
Open now your hearts and share your possessions
so that the church's work is made strong
for the sake of this needy world.

PRAYER OF THANKSGIVING/DEDICATION

Bless in every way, O Lord, the gifts of the people here given.
Enrich the ministries of your people
and make us grateful to be able to let go of the things
we do not, finally, own. **Amen.**

CHARGE

All things are lawful, but not all things are beneficial.   *1 Cor. 6:12*
Listen to the word of the Lord as you move through
    your days.
Trust that the Holy Spirit will guide your choices.
See in each person you meet one for whom Jesus
    gave his life.

BLESSING

The peace of Christ, crucified and risen for all,
go with you this day and always.

Questions for Reflection

Where, in what place, and through what person or persons do you hear
the call of the Lord? Consider it each day this week. Who has awakened
in you a new prayer, a hope, an insight? Give thanks for those persons and
moments as signs of God's love for you.

Household Prayer: Morning

As I rise this day, O God,
I give you thanks for breath and life,
for the people I will see today,
for family, neighbors, and friends,
and for those whose ways are challenging to my serenity.
Help me to give thanks especially
for the people who pull me to new understandings
and show me sides of life that I have not known
or do not welcome.
Urge me to follow you today; in Jesus' name. Amen.

Household Prayer: Evening

As the evening comes and the time for rest draws near, O God,
I give you thanks for another full and mystifying day.
I have not done everything I had hoped to do.
I have not forgiven myself or others as I ought.
I ask now that you, who know me through and through,
will lead me to let go of what I cannot change
and seek anew tomorrow for a more enlightened path.
I long for your guidance and your care.
Guard my sleep, and let me rise renewed; in Jesus' name. Amen.

Third Sunday after the Epiphany

Jonah 3:1–5, 10   1 Corinthians 7:29–31

Psalm 62:5–12   Mark 1:14–20

OPENING WORDS / CALL TO WORSHIP

From God comes my salvation.   *Ps. 62:1–2*
For God alone my soul waits in silence.
God alone is my rock and my salvation.
God is my fortress; I shall never be shaken.

CALL TO CONFESSION

Trusting in the promise of grace,   *Ps. 62:8*
let us pour out our hearts before God.

PRAYER OF CONFESSION

Forgiving God,   *Jonah 3:1–2, 10*
we repent of all the ways we turn from you.
You call, but we do not listen;
you show us your path, but we prefer our own way.
Forgive us, heal us, and lead us back to you,
that we might show mercy to others.
In Jesus' name we pray. Amen.

DECLARATION OF FORGIVENESS

This is the word of the Lord:
in Jesus Christ, you are forgiven by God and given new life.

PRAYER OF THE DAY

The present form of this world is passing away.   *1 Cor. 7:31*
Therefore, help us to keep our focus on you, Lord,
for true power and steadfast love belong to you. **Amen.**   *Ps. 62:11–12*

PRAYER FOR ILLUMINATION

Speak to us your word, O God,
that we may hear Jesus' call to be his disciples. **Amen.**

PRAYERS OF INTERCESSION

God of new visions,
we pray for people highly placed in power,
that they may focus their eyes on you.
And we pray for the lowly victims of power,
that they may also focus their eyes on you.

We pray for those who bless with their lips
but curse with their mouths,   *Ps. 62:4*
including ourselves.

We pray for those who are ill
and those facing the end of life.
Give them the gift of prayer,   *Ps. 62:8*
that they may pour out their hearts to you.

We pray for the church and its leaders,
that we may hear and respond to your call
to be fishers of people.   *Mark 1:17*

Rock of our salvation,
through Christ and your Holy Spirit
bring us into the new world that you are shaping
even as this world is passing away. **Amen.**   *1 Cor. 7:31*

INVITATION TO THE OFFERING

God is our rock and our fortress.
Let us celebrate our salvation
by fearlessly giving a portion
of what has already been given to us.

PRAYER OF THANKSGIVING/DEDICATION

Merciful God, you have saved us for a purpose.
We dedicate these gifts as we dedicate our lives to you,
that you will make us fishers of people.   *Mark 1:17*

CHARGE

Repent and believe the good news that
God is with us and calls us for a purpose!   *Mark 1:14, 17*

BLESSING

May the God of second chances
renew your sense of call
and inspire you to go out and share
the good news of forgiveness and hope!

Question for Reflection

Psalm 62 ends by saying, "God, you repay to all according to their work."
Some of us may find that statement unsettling. Would you rather have God
treat you with the payment you deserve or with the grace that you hope for
in Jesus Christ?

Household Prayer: Morning

Loving God, no matter what I am facing today—
mourning or gladness, buying or selling—
help me to focus on you throughout it all.
Then bring me home safely to you. Amen.

Household Prayer: Evening

Loving God, thank you for the assurance
that I live forgiven and loved by you.
I need your grace and
want to share your grace with others.
As I face this night, help me to pour out my heart to you
and then rest in peace. Amen.

Fourth Sunday after the Epiphany

Deuteronomy 18:15–20   1 Corinthians 8:1–13
Psalm 111   Mark 1:21–28

OPENING WORDS / CALL TO WORSHIP

Come! Let us give thanks to the Lord with whole hearts.   *Ps. 111*
Fear of the Lord is the beginning of wisdom.
Glory be to the One whose wonders are to be remembered.
Fear of the Lord is the beginning of wisdom.
The Lord is gracious and full of compassion.
Fear of the Lord is the beginning of wisdom.
The Lord feeds the righteous with truth.
Fear of the Lord is the beginning of wisdom.
Come! Let us give thanks to God.

CALL TO CONFESSION

The One who pardons, heals, and strengthens all who repent
calls us to name our failings and our hopes.
Let us confess our sin in the presence of God and one another.

PRAYER OF CONFESSION

Holy and all-powerful God,
who commands all spirits,
comforts those in distress,
and casts out destructive forces,
we confess that we are unable to do your will.
We protect what is familiar
and reject what is unknown.
We admire those with courage
but excuse ourselves when we falter from the truth.
We forget that you are always with us,
and that with you all things are possible.

Forgive us, lead us, make us new.
**Remove our desire to heed false prophets,
and show us your way;
in the name of the Father, Son, and Holy Spirit,
one God, Mother of us all. Amen.**

DECLARATION OF FORGIVENESS

The God who made you and knows your every thought
hears you now and forgives you all your sin.
You have been redeemed through Jesus Christ,
God's Son, our Savior, who is Alpha and Omega, all in all.

PRAYER OF THE DAY

Almighty God, Light from Light,
who commands the universe and all that is made,
your Word is the power that makes whole what is broken,
the force of good, and the food of peace.
Teach us now as you taught in the synagogue.
Heal us now so that in all that we say and do,
the freedom we have in you may be for others, too;
in Jesus' name we pray. **Amen.**

PRAYER FOR ILLUMINATION

Holy Spirit, your people call out for understanding.
Bring to our yearning hearts and minds
the truth of your Word; in Jesus' name. **Amen.**

PRAYERS OF INTERCESSION

Let us pray for the needs of the world, saying,
Hear us, O God, your mercy is great.

For the healing of Earth and all its creatures;
hear us, O God, **your mercy is great.**

For the church's willingness to cast out demons in its midst,
for congregations that are in turmoil,
for the healing of divisions between the followers of Christ Jesus;
hear us, O God, **your mercy is great.**

For leaders of nations,
for those who have great wealth,
for those who have too much power,
for those who have destructive weapons,
and for those who have none;
hear us, O God, **your mercy is great.**

For those who are victims of others' idolatry,
for children who have no one to listen to their cries for food and shelter,
for parents who cannot answer the needs of their children,
for peacemakers and diplomats,
for those who give through charities,
and for those who use the law
to make policies for the greater good;
hear us, O God, **your mercy is great.**

For all who are in pain and in need of care,
especially those we name now aloud or silently, . . .
[A time of silence is kept.]
hear us, O God, **your mercy is great.**

For the wisdom to fear you rightly,
the power to withstand changes in our own lives
that bring us closer to you,
for the ability to give thanks for the people
who have brought us to this time—
our ancestors, teachers, pastors, and the martyrs of every age;
hear us, O God, **your mercy is great.**

Into your hands we commend all those for whom we pray
and those it would be easy to forget.
We ask your blessing on all your people,
that we may come at last to the truth
around your banquet table that has no end;
through Christ Jesus, our Lord,
who lives and reigns with you and the Holy Spirit,
one God, now and forever. **Amen.**

INVITATION TO THE OFFERING

Do not let idols grow and multiply in your hands,
but give of yourselves, your time, and your possessions
out of love for this creation
and honor toward what you have been given.

PRAYER OF THANKSGIVING/DEDICATION

For Earth, which you have molded,
for creatures and animals, plants, water, air, and fire,
for Jesus who died and rose again,
for the breath of life,
we give you thanks, O God.
Let these gifts be used for good wherever there is need,
in the name of all that you have first given us,
especially Christ Jesus, your Son, our Savior. **Amen.**

CHARGE

Go out from this place to a world fully known by God.
Where there is fear, remember the authority of Christ Jesus.
Where there is need of love, give it.
Where there is pain, bring peace.
For you are loved by the One who redeems,
and freed to live by the Word of life.

BLESSING

Go in peace with the knowledge that God's power
is given to the church, the body of Christ,
for the sake of the life of the world.

Questions for Reflection

What is the name of the demon, the spirit, the idolatry you carry? If you
can think of this answer as many "troubles," try to find the root cause,
a name to give to that which needs to be cast out. The answer may take
different forms throughout the week. You may also consider the same
question with regard to your family and to this nation. What is the Holy
One casting out today in your presence?

Household Prayer: Morning

In the light of your new day, O God,
I rise to greet you always on the path in front of me.
Let me follow with integrity where you will lead.
Give me courage to know the difference
between what is false and what is true.
Teach me to love my neighbor as you love me. Amen.

Household Prayer: Evening

Heavenly Father, you are the power above all powers,
the healer who knows our every need.
You have guided me throughout this day
and now give me sleep to renew my tired body and mind.
Guard me and keep me in your care. Amen.

Fifth Sunday after the Epiphany

Isaiah 40:21–31   1 Corinthians 9:16–23
Psalm 147:1–11, 20c   Mark 1:29–39

OPENING WORDS / CALL TO WORSHIP

Have we not known? Have we not heard?   *Isa. 40:21*
Has it not been told to us since the beginning?
Those who wait for the Lord shall renew their strength;   *Isa. 40:31*
they shall mount up with wings like eagles;
they shall run and not be weary;
they shall walk and not faint.

CALL TO CONFESSION

We fool ourselves if we think
that our ways are hidden from God.
Therefore let us confess our sin,
trusting in the mercy of God our Maker.

PRAYER OF CONFESSION

God, you are everlasting,
the creator of all that is.
Your understanding is beyond measure.   *Ps. 147:5*
We confess to you that we have
sinned against you and our neighbors.
In your compassion, forgive us,
for we place our hope in your steadfast love.   *Ps. 147:11*

DECLARATION OF FORGIVENESS

Praise the Lord!
Our God heals the brokenhearted   *Ps. 147:3*
and binds up our wounds.

God takes pleasure in those
who place their trust in God's grace.
In Jesus Christ we are forgiven.

PRAYER OF THE DAY

Gracious God, you call us to follow Christ
and spread the good news of your love for all people.
Help us to become all things to all people   *1 Cor. 9:22*
that we might reach many with your good news. **Amen.**

PRAYER FOR ILLUMINATION

Holy God, speak to us
what has been told from the beginning,
your Word that is the foundation of the world. **Amen.**   *Isa. 40:21*

PRAYERS OF INTERCESSION

God of the universe,
you sit above the circle of the earth,   *Isa. 40:21–22*
and so we pray for the oceans and mountains,
inland water and the air we breathe.
Save and protect them, we pray.

Since the beginning of our faith,
we have looked to you to gather the outcasts,
heal the brokenhearted and bind up their wounds.   *Ps. 147:2–3*
So we pray for the poor of the world,
the sick and the lonely.   ·

God, you build up Jerusalem,   *Ps. 147:2*
and so we pray for our country,
for all the countries of the world,
and for all of our leaders.
May we all come to see that your delight
is not in the strength of the military   *Ps. 147:10*
but in those who hope in your steadfast love.   *Ps. 147:11*

How good it is to sing praises to you, O God.   *Ps. 147:1*
We pray for your church,
here and around the world.
Empower us to go from town to town,   *Mark 1:38–39*
proclaiming the message of Christ.

Everlasting God, Creator of the ends of the earth,   *Isa. 40:28*
we bless you, for you are gracious.   *Ps. 147:1*
Through Christ, with Christ, in Christ,
in the unity of the Holy Spirit,
all glory and honor are yours, now and forever. **Amen.**

INVITATION TO THE OFFERING

Let us give thanks to God
by giving our tithes and offerings.

PRAYER OF THANKSGIVING/DEDICATION

We sing to you, God, with thanksgiving,
making melody to you with our praise.   *Ps. 147:7*
Use these gifts to spread your gospel near and far,
for the sake of your Son, Jesus Christ. **Amen.**

CHARGE

Let us spread the gospel free of charge.   *1 Cor. 9:18*

BLESSING

May the Spirit of Jesus   *Mark 1:31*
take your hand and lift you up
so that you may be of service to others.

Question for Reflection

What does Paul mean when he says that he became all things to all people
so that he could save some (1 Cor. 9:22)?

Household Prayer: Morning

In the morning, while it was still very dark,
Jesus got up and went out to a deserted place,
     and there he prayed.   *Mark 1:35*
As I turn to you in prayer this morning, God,
bless me with a sense of purpose.
As I go out into this day, show me what I am to do. Amen.

Everlasting God, you have been here
from the foundations of the earth.
I give to you this day now ending,
with all its gifts and failings.
As I rest through the night,
renew my strength and, in my dreams,
lift me up on the wings of eagles. Amen.

Sixth Sunday after the Epiphany

2 Kings 5:1–14   1 Corinthians 9:24–27
Psalm 30   Mark 1:40–45

OPENING WORDS / CALL TO WORSHIP

O Lord, our God, we cry to you and you restore our health.   *Ps. 30:2*
Our healer washes us in the waters of baptism,
cleanses us from all that enslaves,
and gives us peace.
O Lord, our God, we will give you thanks forever.   *Ps. 30:12*

CALL TO CONFESSION

In obedience to God's command to repent,
let us lay before God and one another our need
    for forgiveness,
that we might receive healing mercy.

PRAYER OF CONFESSION

Merciful God, we confess that without you, we are not whole.
Forgive our foolish ways,
reform our prideful selves,
make us listen to the way of peace,
remove from us the disbelief to which we cling.
You are the One who liberates with a word
and nourishes us with your own bruised body.
Give us thankful hearts as we come to the waters of life
with trust and hope. Amen.

DECLARATION OF FORGIVENESS

The God who knows you through and through,
whose own body and blood were given for your freedom,
who calls you to renewal every day,

67

hears your repentance and by grace has made you clean.
As a called and ordained minister of the church of Christ,
I declare to you the forgiveness of all your sins,
in the name of the Holy Trinity, one God, now and forever.

PRAYER OF THE DAY

Holy God, you choose for us goodness and wholeness.
You look on us with love and stretch out your hand.
Give us ears to hear what you command so that,
ready to do as you desire, we may see your guidance
and protection and come to love our neighbors as ourselves;
in the name of the One who heals by dying, Jesus our Savior. **Amen.**

PRAYER FOR ILLUMINATION

Give us ears, O God, to hear your word
beyond our own expectations.
Let your Holy Spirit infuse us with insight,
in the light of your continued Epiphany in our midst.
In Jesus' name we pray. **Amen.**

PRAYERS OF INTERCESSION

Living in the light of Christ,
who reveals both our lives and God's abundant love,
let us pray for the church, those in need,
and all of God's creation, saying,
Hear us, O God; your mercy is great.

God of new life,
you renew us daily through your baptismal promises.
Guide us in all we do,
that your power will shine in our words and deeds.
Hear us, O God; **your mercy is great.**

We pray for Earth,
for the health of all bodies of water,
for [name a local body of water, source of local water, or watershed],
and for all rivers and streams,
that in the clear, clean waters you have created for us to drink and use,
we may see your love for all your creatures.
Hear us, O God; **your mercy is great.**

For all who live directly by the bounty of earth:
for those who sow seeds, raise livestock, and catch fish;
for people who work in processing plants and factories
or manufacture farm implements;
for people who pack and haul and sell us
their vegetables, fruits, and meats.
Bless them in their labor
for the sake of all who depend on them for food.
Hear us, O God; **your mercy is great.**

For all governments:
for *[name the U.S. president and your state's governor],*
for city councils, for county commissioners, for mayors,
and for all who vote.
Give wisdom to our people,
that we will choose leaders who will serve the needs of everyone.
Hear us, O God; **your mercy is great.**

For children throughout the world:
for good schools and compassionate teachers,
for healthy homes,
for clothing, food, and shelter enough that they can thrive and grow;
for friends and neighbors, aunts and uncles, grandparents and parents
who watch well over little ones,
that their joy in this world be complete.
Hear us, O God; **your mercy is great.**

For all people who are in distress:
those who are hurting, those who worry,
those who are sick, those in need of a friend;
for all on the prayer list of this congregation;
for all whose names are known only to you.
Hear us, O God; **your mercy is great.**

Hear now the concerns of this body, spoken silently or aloud. . . .
[A time of silence is kept.]
Hear us, O God; **your mercy is great.**

We remember with gratitude for their witness
the saints we commemorate this coming week:

[name those who in the coming week the church commemorates].
Help us to live in honor of their faith.
Hear us, O God; **your mercy is great.**

Into your hands, gracious God,
we commend all for whom we pray, trusting in your mercy;
through Jesus Christ, our Savior. **Amen.**

INVITATION TO THE OFFERING
As Elisha, the prophet, gave to Naaman, the general, in his need,
let us give what we can for the sake of others,
that all may be fed and clothed and sheltered,
that all may hear the truth and be made free.

PRAYER OF THANKSGIVING/DEDICATION
For your gifts that live all around us in creation, O God,
we give you thanks.
For your gifts that come from the servanthood
    of your Son, O God,
we give you praise.
For the gifts that arise in our daily lives
    through the work of your Holy Spirit, O God,
we give you thanks.
Make these gifts flourish on earth to your glory. **Amen.**

CHARGE
Go as the young servant of Naaman this day,
filled with the truth of the prophet's word that there is healing
for the least and the greatest among us.
Speak peace,
teach kindness,
be glad.

BLESSING
May God's blessings attend you this and every day.
You are not alone.
Go in peace.

Question for Reflection

What simple kindness each day this week has shown you a glimpse of God's everlasting, steadfast love?

Household Prayer: Morning

Holy One, who greets me in the morning and gives me rest at night,
let me see you in the people I meet today.
Let me hear your voice in the sounds that surround me.
Let me heed your call to breathe deeply
when I am confused or distressed.
Let me speak kindly to my neighbors this day.
Be my guide and shield,
in the name of Christ Jesus,
who goes before me every step. Amen.

Household Prayer: Evening

Holy One, who calms my troubled mind as the evening comes,
I give you thanks for the richness of this day:
for the work I have had to do,
for the home that offers me a place to rest,
for the friends and family who have touched me in the last hours,
and for the people of your church in every land whose prayers—
unknown to me—are yet a part of my life through you.
Bless your people everywhere, and bless me, too,
as I lay down to sleep; in Jesus' name, I pray. Amen.

Seventh Sunday after the Epiphany

Isaiah 43:18–25   2 Corinthians 1:18–22
Psalm 41   Mark 2:1–12

OPENING WORDS / CALL TO WORSHIP

Do not remember the former things or consider the
    things of old.   *Isa. 43:18–19*
I am about to do a new thing, says our God.
Now it springs forth—do you not perceive it?
I will make a way in the wilderness and rivers
    in the desert.   *Isa. 43:20–21*
For I will give drink to my chosen people,
the people I formed for myself so that they might
    declare my praise!

CALL TO CONFESSION

Our God has been so gracious to us.
Let us confess to God and each other
the ways in which we have failed to behave
with the same graciousness.

PRAYER OF CONFESSION

Holy One, we have not remembered the poor,   *Ps. 41:1*
and so we fear that you will not remember us
in our time of need.
With the psalmist we pray,
O Lord, be gracious to me;   *Ps. 41:4*
heal me, for I have sinned against you.
In Jesus' name we ask it. Amen.

DECLARATION OF FORGIVENESS

Our God has been gracious to us *Ps. 41:10, 12*
and has raised us up.
God has upheld us and
placed us in God's presence forever.
Blessed be the Lord, the God of Israel, *Ps. 41:13*
from everlasting to everlasting. Amen and amen!

PRAYER OF THE DAY

Great Physician, we thank you for the faith of others
that enables our own healing.
Send us such sisters and brothers
when we are in need,
and help us to be friends who help others in need;
through Jesus Christ. **Amen.**

PRAYER FOR ILLUMINATION

Holy God, by your Spirit
speak to us your resounding yes! *2 Cor. 1:20*
as we listen to your Word. **Amen.**

PRAYERS OF INTERCESSION

God, in the beginning you created
the heavens and the earth.
Preserve and sustain your creation, we pray.

We pray for the poor and the outcasts, *Ps. 41:1*
for you are their God.
Deliver them when they are in trouble.
Strengthen those who work for the poor, *Ps. 41:2–3*
and those who care for the sick and infirm.
Sustain those who suffer and heal all their infirmities.

We pray for political and religious leaders
when they utter empty words *Ps. 41:6*
while their hearts gather mischief.
Lord, bring them back to integrity
and into your presence. *Ps. 41:12*

We grow weary under the burden
of the sins of the world.
Have mercy on us.

Now in the name of your son, Jesus Christ,
in whom your word is always yes,   *2 Cor. 1:20*
and under the seal of the Holy Spirit,   *2 Cor. 1:22*
we praise your name and say:
Amen to the glory of God!   *2 Cor. 1:20*

INVITATION TO THE OFFERING
God gives a way in the wilderness
and gives rivers in the desert.   *Isa. 43:19*
Let us give generously so that
many may find the way of the Lord.

PRAYER OF THANKSGIVING/DEDICATION
God, you say yes to each one of us,   *2 Cor. 1:20*
affirming your promises to us.
And so we say yes to you
by dedicating these offerings
to the expansion of your commonwealth on earth,
for the sake of your Son, Jesus Christ. **Amen.**

CHARGE
God is doing a new thing—be part of it!   *Isa. 43:19*

BLESSING
May you have Spirit-filled friends
who would dig through a thatched roof for you   *Mark 2:4*
and bring you into the presence of Jesus.
And may you hear Christ say to you,
"Pick up your mat and walk!"   *Mark 2:9*

Questions for Reflection

What are some of the "new things" that you see God doing in our world
today? How are you a part of them? How do you resist them?

Household Prayer: Morning

O God, there are days when I feel that my life is just a mindless routine,
that I am stuck in a rut.
Help me not to focus so much on "the former things, the things of old."
Reveal to me, through the course of this day,
what new things God is doing in my life
and in the world around me.
Open my eyes to how I can take part in those new things today. Amen.

Household Prayer: Evening

Creator of life and new life,
thank you for once again
making a way for me through this day.
Uphold me in my integrity,
and let me rest this night in your presence.
With the seal of your Holy Spirit on my heart,
and thinking of ways that Christ said
yes to me today,
I will rest in your love for me. Amen.

Eighth Sunday after the Epiphany

Hosea 2:14–20   2 Corinthians 3:1–6
Psalm 103:1–13, 22   Mark 2:13–22

OPENING WORDS / CALL TO WORSHIP
Jesus says, "Follow me."   *Mark 2:14*
We arise and follow. Praise the Lord.

CALL TO CONFESSION
Jesus declares that those who are well have no need
    of a physician,   *Mark 2:17*
but those who are sick;
Christ calls not the righteous but sinners.
Disciples of Jesus, let us confess our sins before God.

PRAYER OF CONFESSION
Merciful God,
your love for us is undivided,   *Hos. 2:14–20*
but we confess that we have been unfaithful
    in our devotion to you.
Our affections stray to false gods of money
    and power.
Our commitments fracture among the demands
    of work and family.
Our loyalties spread across the obligations
    of social class and nation.
Forgive us, we pray.
Reconcile our wandering hearts and restore us
    to faithfulness.
Ground us in your righteous covenant
that we may know to whom we belong,
live as your committed partner,
and honor you as our gracious Lord. Amen.

DECLARATION OF FORGIVENESS

The Lord is merciful and gracious,   *Ps. 103:8*
slow to anger and abounding in steadfast love.
In the name of Jesus Christ, you are forgiven.
Thanks be to God.

PRAYER OF THE DAY

Generous God,
whose love embraces the sinner and challenges
    the self-righteous,   *Mark 2:13–22*
enable us to hear the call of discipleship,
trusting not in our worthiness
but in the healing love of Jesus Christ,
    the Great Physician. **Amen.**

PRAYER FOR ILLUMINATION

Spirit of the Living God,
write your Word on the tablets of our hearts,   *2 Cor. 3:2–3*
that we may be your letter to the world,
showing forth the good news of Jesus Christ. **Amen.**

PRAYERS OF INTERCESSION

With the confidence of God's children, let us pray, saying,
God, in your mercy, hear our prayer.

Generous God, in Christ you embrace people
of every time and place.
For the holy church of God,
for those who lead the ministry of the church,
and for all who follow the way of Jesus,
that through the witness of Jesus' disciples
the expansive love of God may be known in all the world,
God, in your mercy, **hear our prayer.**

Generous God, in kindness you bring justice
    to the oppressed.   *Ps. 103:6*
For nations to live in harmony with each other
and for those in authority to exercise justice for the poor,
that oppression may end and peace abound,
God, in your mercy, **hear our prayer.**

Generous God, you satisfy us with good
    as long as we live.   *Ps. 103:5*
For our city *[town]* and for all who live here,
that our neighborhoods may promote the flourishing
of young and old, infant and elderly,
and every home know the goodness of human care,
God, in your mercy, **hear our prayer.**

Generous God, in love you brought forth creation.
For our natural world,
that the gardens of earth may be fruitful
and humanity dwell in harmony with the land,
God, in your mercy, **hear our prayer.**

Generous God, you give justice to the oppressed.   *Ps. 103:6*
For those who suffer cruel systems of government
or endure the hardship of war,
that they may receive protection from violence,
release from oppression,
and freedom to pursue wholesome work,
God, in your mercy, **hear our prayer.**

Generous God, you heal us in body and soul.
For those who suffer illness,
that they may be restored to wholeness of life
and fullness of spirit,
God, in your mercy, **hear our prayer.**

Generous God,
you know our need and our weakness in asking.
As our compassionate Parent,   *Ps. 103:13*
receive our prayers and grant them according to
    your merciful goodness
made known to us in Jesus Christ by the power
    of the Holy Spirit. **Amen.**

INVITATION TO THE OFFERING
Remembering all God's benefits to us,   *Ps. 103:2*
let us offer ourselves and our gifts in humble service.

PRAYER OF THANKSGIVING/DEDICATION

Loving God,
we give you thanks for the light of the world, Jesus Christ.
Receive the gifts we offer in union with Christ,
that we may be ministers of his new covenant   *2 Cor. 3:6*
through the power of the life-giving Spirit. **Amen.**

CHARGE

Go forth into the world
as a disciple of Jesus Christ
to live the good news.

BLESSING

May the steadfast love of God renew you,
the word of Jesus Christ guide you,
and the power of the Holy Spirit strengthen you,
now and forever.

Question for Reflection

Jesus associated with sinners and tax collectors, people who had a terrible
reputation among polite society. Not only did he call them into his
fellowship, he went to their places of business and ate in their homes. He
declared, "I have come to call not the righteous but sinners" (Mark 2:17).
How does the church today interact with those who are publicly known as
"sinners"?

Household Prayer: Morning

Lord Jesus,
lest I trust in my own righteousness,
keep me mindful of my faults and my need of your grace;
remove from my heart any prejudice
that would hinder me from sharing the good news with others;
and allow me to sit at table with you
in the company of the sinners
you have called to be your disciples. Amen.

Household Prayer: Evening

God, like a worried child, I wonder, "Do you love me?"
And you answer,
"As the heavens are high above the earth, so great is my love for you."
Thank you, God, for helping me to imagine
your immeasurable love. Amen.

Ninth Sunday after the Epiphany

Deuteronomy 5:12–15   2 Corinthians 4:5–12
Psalm 81:1–10   Mark 2:23–3:6

OPENING WORDS / CALL TO WORSHIP
Sing joyful songs to God, our Savior.   *Deut. 5:15; Ps. 81:1–3*
Remember the Lord, who set us free.
Blow the trumpet; sound the tambourine!
Remember the Lord, the God of life.

CALL TO CONFESSION
[Pouring water into the font]
In our distress, we call to the Lord,   *Ps. 81:7*
who rescues us.
Whether we are drowning in sin
or thirsty for salvation,
God is ready to save.
Rejoicing in God's grace,
let us confess our sin.

PRAYER OF CONFESSION
God of freedom, have mercy on us.   *Deut. 5:12–15;*
We enjoy idle pleasures   *Mark 2:23–3:6*
and pursue lives of leisure
while others stoop to serve us
and struggle to support themselves.
We enact rules and regulations
that benefit the wealthy
at the expense of basic needs—
human health and daily bread.
Forgive us.

81

Set us free to serve you
and to seek the liberation of all;
through Jesus Christ our Lord. Amen.

DECLARATION OF FORGIVENESS

[Lifting water from the font]
Hear the promise of the Lord: *Ps. 81:10*
I am the Holy One, your God,
who brought you up out of the land of Egypt.
Open your mouth wide, and I will fill it.

Like weary travelers in the wilderness,
let us drink deeply of God's grace.
In Jesus Christ, we are forgiven.
Thanks be to God.

PRAYER OF THE DAY

God of Sunday and Sabbath,   *Deut. 5:12–15; 2 Cor. 4:5–12;*
we praise you for your work of creation   *Mark 2:23–3:6*
and give thanks for your gift of rest.
By the power of your Word and Spirit,
let there be a new creation here among us—
a place where all may enjoy
your good gifts of life and freedom;
through Jesus Christ our Lord. **Amen.**

PRAYER FOR ILLUMINATION

Holy God, we give thanks for your Word   *2 Cor. 4:5, 7*
speaking through Scripture,
like a treasure in clay jars.
Let us carry these words with us
and live as vessels of your truth,
proclaiming the good news of life
in Jesus Christ our Lord. **Amen.**

PRAYERS OF INTERCESSION

Let us pray for the health of the church   *2 Cor. 4:11; Mark 3:5*
and the healing of the world, saying,
To you, Lord God,
we stretch out our hands.

We pray for the church. . . .
Set us free from worldly passions;
give us passion for heavenly things:
to proclaim Jesus Christ as Lord
and to serve others, for Jesus' sake.
To you, Lord God,
we stretch out our hands.

We pray for the world. . . .
Let the earth have Sabbath rest:
an end to war and oppression,
destruction and pollution,
corruption and greed.
To you, Lord God,
we stretch out our hands.

We pray for this community. . . .
Give rest to those who labor
and provide work for the unemployed
so that all may have an equal share
of the fullness of life you offer.
To you, Lord God,
we stretch out our hands.

We pray for loved ones. . . .
Give healing to those who are afflicted,
wisdom to those who are perplexed,
peace to those who are persecuted,
and new life to those who are struck down.
To you, Lord God,
we stretch out our hands.

Restore us, Lord God.
Giver of life, make us whole
so that the life and light of Jesus Christ
may be visible in us,
and the world may see your glory;
in your holy name we pray. **Amen.**

INVITATION TO THE OFFERING

Jesus said: The Sabbath was made for humankind.   *Mark 2:27–28*
The gifts of God are meant
for human life and flourishing.

Therefore, let us offer the gifts of our lives
to the Lord and giver of all life.

PRAYER OF THANKSGIVING/DEDICATION

We give you thanks, O God,   *2 Cor. 4:7*
for every blessing you provide—
life, health, community, freedom—
and above all, the treasure of life in Christ.
By your Spirit, empower us
to extend these blessings to others
for the sake of Jesus Christ our Lord. **Amen.**

CHARGE

For freedom Christ has set us free.   *Gal. 5:1; Deut. 5:15*
Go forth to love and serve the Lord
in freedom. **Amen.**

BLESSING

May the blessing of the Lord,   *Deut. 5:15; Mark 2:28*
the liberating giver of life,
be with you all,
this day and always. **Alleluia!**

Questions for Reflection

Why did Jesus find himself in conflict with the religious authorities over
the keeping of the Sabbath (Mark 2:23–3:6; cf. Deut. 5:12–15)? What does
it mean that "the sabbath was made for humankind, and not humankind
for the sabbath" (Mark 2:27)? Can you think of situations in which the laws
of church or state come into conflict with the values of human health and
well-being? How do you imagine Jesus might address such situations?

Household Prayer: Morning

God of daily bread,   *2 Cor. 4:6; Mark 2:23, 3:5*
I stretch out my hands to you:
provide for me
the things I need this day
so that I may live
to share the light of Jesus. Amen.

Household Prayer: Evening

God of Sabbath rest,   *Deut. 5:15; 2 Cor. 4:6*
now stretch out your arms to me:
provide for me
the peace I need this night
so that I may dream
about the light of Jesus. Amen.

Transfiguration Sunday
(Last Sunday before Lent)

2 Kings 2:1–12   2 Corinthians 4:3–6
Psalm 50:1–6   Mark 9:2–9

OPENING WORDS / CALL TO WORSHIP

The glory of God shines   *Ps. 50:1, 3; 2 Cor. 4:6;*
like a consuming fire.   *Mark 9:7*
We have seen the glory of God
in the face of Jesus Christ.
The voice of God thunders
like a mighty storm.
Out of the cloud, God speaks:
This is my beloved Son; listen to him!

CALL TO CONFESSION

[Pouring water into the font]
God alone is righteous;   *Ps. 50:2, 6*
God alone is perfect;
God alone is judge.
Yet this holy, righteous God
comes to us in love, to save us.
Rejoicing in God's grace,
let us confess our sin.

PRAYER OF CONFESSION

God of all glory, beauty, and grace,   *2 Cor. 4:3–6; Mark 9:2–9*
we have tried to hide from you—
to hide our faces, to hide our sin—
yet you have never hidden your love for us.
We have tried to search for you—
in temples, in clouds, on mountaintops—

yet you have already revealed yourself to us
in the face of Jesus Christ.
Forgive us, and transform us
so that our lives may shine
with your glory, beauty, and grace;
through Jesus Christ our Lord. Amen.

DECLARATION OF FORGIVENESS

[Lifting water from the font]

Our God comes and does not keep silence;   *Ps. 50:3; Mark 9:7*
God speaks to us with grace and love,
saying: You are my beloved child.

This is the good news of the gospel:
In Jesus Christ we are forgiven.
Thanks be to God.

PRAYER OF THE DAY

Holy and mighty God,   *Ps. 50:1, 5; Mark 9:7*
gather us among your faithful ones,
the people of your covenant,
to stand in the light of your glory
and listen for the word of the Lord,
Jesus Christ our Savior. **Amen.**

PRAYER FOR ILLUMINATION

Speak to us, O Lord our God,   *Ps. 50:1; 2 Cor. 4:6;*
and let the fire of your Spirit   *Mark 9:4*
burn brightly in our hearts.
Open our minds to receive
the wisdom of the law,
the hope of the prophets,
and the life of the gospel:
Jesus Christ, your living Word. **Amen.**

PRAYERS OF INTERCESSION

Mighty and merciful one,   *Ps. 50:1–3; 2 Kgs. 2:9–10;*
you have come to us in glory;   *Mark 2:9, 7*
now we come to you in prayer, saying,
Lord, by your Spirit,
grant what we ask.

We pray for your glorious creation. . . .
Stamp out fires of destruction,
drive away clouds of pollution,
and restore the beauty of this world.
Lord, by your Spirit,
grant what we ask.

We pray for the body of Christ. . . .
Open our hearts in faith,
enlighten our minds with knowledge,
and strengthen us to proclaim the gospel.
Lord, by your Spirit,
grant what we ask.

We pray for the people of all nations. . . .
Show the nations your vision of justice,
offer the leaders your mantle of wisdom,
and give the people your blessing of peace.
Lord, by your Spirit,
grant what we ask.

We pray for those who are perishing. . . .
Feed those who are starving,
comfort those who are suffering,
and receive the dying into your arms.
Lord, by your Spirit,
grant what we ask.

We pray for those whom we love. . . .
Bless our families, friends, and neighbors,
help them in times of trouble,
and be near when they are afraid.
Lord, by your Spirit,
grant what we ask.

Holy One, make us ready for the day
when this world is transfigured,
transformed, made new—
when all things will shine
in the dazzling light of your glory;
through Jesus Christ our Lord. **Amen.**

INVITATION TO THE OFFERING

The God who speaks   *Ps. 50:1*
and summons the earth into being
now speaks to us,
calling us to offer up our lives
as a sacrifice of praise.

PRAYER OF THANKSGIVING/DEDICATION

Gracious God, we give you thanks   *2 Cor. 4:6*
for the light of love around us
and the fire of faith within us.
As we go forth from this place
let our lives reflect the One
who is the image of your glory:
Jesus Christ, the light of the world. **Amen.**

CHARGE

Now go and tell the good news: *Mark 9:9*
the Lord of life and light is with us;
Jesus Christ is risen from the dead. **Amen.**

BLESSING

The very face of God shines upon you   *Ps. 50:2*
with beauty, blessing, and peace. **Alleluia!**

Questions for Reflection

The Old Testament reading for today presents Elijah as a "new Moses"—
striking the Jordan with his mantle and causing its waters to part so that
he and Elisha could pass through on dry ground (2 Kgs. 2:8). The Gospel
reading builds on this comparison by placing Moses and Elijah together
at Jesus' transfiguration (Mark 9:4). There is also a parent-child dynamic
in each of these passages. Elisha asks to receive a "double share" of Elijah's
spirit (2 Kgs. 2:9)—the appointed inheritance of a firstborn son (see Deut.
21:17). At the transfiguration, God's voice from the cloud bestows on Jesus
the mantle of divine authority: "This is my Son, the Beloved; listen to
him!" What do these constellations of relationships suggest to you? How
do they help you to understand the transfiguration of Jesus? How is Jesus
a fulfillment of the law (Moses) and the prophets (Elijah)? (See also Luke
24:44.) How is Jesus revealed to be God's Son, and what does that mean for
us? (See also Luke 3:22, 38.)

Household Prayer: Morning

God of glory, I greet you
at the dawning of this day.
Let my life proclaim Christ Jesus
and the good news of the gospel
from the rising of the sun to its setting;
to the glory of your name. Amen.

Household Prayer: Evening

God of glory, I greet you
at the ending of this day.
Overshadow me with your peace
so that I may rest in your presence
from the setting of the sun to its rising;
to the glory of your name. Amen.

Ash Wednesday

Joel 2:1–2, 12–17   2 Corinthians 5:20b–6:10
    or Isaiah 58:1–12
Psalm 51:1–17   Matthew 6:1–6, 16–21

CALL TO WORSHIP / OPENING WORDS

Blow the trumpet in Zion; sound the alarm upon
    the holy mountain!   *Joel 2:1*
Let everyone tremble, for the day of the Lord is near.

CALL TO CONFESSION

The prophet Joel cried out: *Joel 2:12–13*
Return to the Lord with all your heart,
with fasting, with weeping, and with mourning;
rend your hearts and not your clothing.
For God is gracious and merciful, slow to anger,
and abounding in steadfast love.
Let us confess our sins and repent of all unrighteousness.

PRAYER OF CONFESSION

Merciful God,   *Isa. 58:4–7*
we confess that we have been a rebellious people.
We have broken your covenant,
and we have tolerated injustice in our land.
We have not shared our food with the hungry,
we have not sheltered the homeless,
and we have not aided the destitute.
We quarrel and fight among ourselves,
and we use religion to cover our deceit.
We have become a mockery of our heritage;   *Joel 2:17*
the world looks at us and asks, Where is their God?
Forgive us, O God.

Subdue our rebellious hearts
and restore in us the light of salvation;
through Jesus Christ, our Lord. Amen.

DECLARATION OF FORGIVENESS

If you remove the yoke from among you,   *Isa. 58:9b–10*
the pointing of the finger, the speaking of evil,
if you offer your food to the hungry and satisfy
    the needs of the afflicted,
then your light shall rise in the darkness and your gloom
    be like the noonday.
In the name of Jesus Christ,
know that you are forgiven and rejoice.
Thanks be to God.

PRAYER OF THE DAY

God of Righteousness,   *Matt. 6:18–20*
you see the secret acts of our devotion
and know the hidden motives of our hearts.
Confirm in us a spirit of humble obedience,
that without regard to earthly honor
we may live as your faithful children
and receive the treasure of eternal life
with Jesus Christ our Lord. **Amen.**

PRAYER FOR ILLUMINATION

By the illumination of your Holy Spirit, O God,
open our hearts that we may hear your Word
and amend our lives;
through Jesus Christ. **Amen.**

BLESSING OF ASHES

Bless, O God, these ashes and those who receive them.
Let them be for us a reminder of our mortality,
a call to sincere repentance,
and a testimony to your abundant mercy
in Jesus Christ. **Amen.**

PRAYERS OF INTERCESSION

Trusting in God's righteousness,
let us pray for the world and for our needs, saying,
Holy God, hear our prayer.

For the church, that in this season of fasting and repentance
the people of God, with sincere hearts,
may amend their lives and obey the gospel,
Holy God, **hear our prayer.**

For all pastors and teachers,
that they may lead the church by humble example
and give public witness without concern for earthly reward,
Holy God, **hear our prayer.**

For peace among the nations
and integrity within the governments,
Holy God, **hear our prayer.**

For our city *[town]* and for all who live here,
that neighborhoods may be places of hospitality and care,
Holy God, **hear our prayer.**

For the poor and the oppressed,
that they may find deliverance from their distress,
and for all who seek to alleviate human suffering,
Holy God, **hear our prayer.**

For those who suffer illness of mind or body
and for those who care for them,
that they may be healed of disease and know the joy
    of abundant life,
Holy God, **hear our prayer.**

For these concerns and those known only to you, Holy God,
we pray in the name of Jesus Christ our Lord. **Amen.**

INVITATION TO THE OFFERING

Jesus said, whenever you give alms, do not sound
    a trumpet before you,   *Matt. 6:2*
as the hypocrites do in the synagogues and in the streets
so that they may be praised by others.
With humble hearts, let us make our offering to God.

PRAYER OF THANKSGIVING/DEDICATION

Holy God, with these gifts we thank you   *Matt. 6:19–21*
for the imperishable treasure of eternal life
and dedicate the work of our hands
to the ministry of Jesus Christ,
in whose name we pray. **Amen.**

CHARGE

Disciples of Jesus,   *Isa. 58:6–7*
observe a Holy Lent:
loose the bonds of injustice,
break the yoke of oppression,
feed the hungry,
shelter the poor.

BLESSING

With the blessing of God our maker,   *Isa. 58:8*
Christ our redeemer, and the Spirit our sustainer,
receive the promise of Isaiah:
Your light shall break forth like the dawn,
and your healing shall spring up quickly;
God your protector shall go before you,
and the glory of the Lord shall be your rear guard.

Question for Reflection

In today's Gospel reading from the Sermon on the Mount, Jesus teaches his disciples to do acts of piety in secret (Matt. 6:1–6, 16–21). However, in an earlier part of the Sermon on the Mount, Jesus instructs his disciples, "Let your light shine before others, so that they may see your good works and give glory to your Father in heaven" (Matt. 5:16). How do you manage this paradox in your life?

Household Prayer: Morning

Lord Jesus,
help me be your disciple today.
If I receive rebuke from anyone, let me suffer it with grace.
If I receive commendation, let me accept it without vanity.
Strengthen my hope in the treasure that endures,
that I may know with you the joy of heaven. Amen.

Household Prayer: Evening

O God, my heart has been stained with the sin of this world;
my spirit is weary and my joy has grown dim.
With the psalmist I pray:
Create in me a clean heart, O God,
and put a new and right spirit within me.
Do not cast me away from your presence,
and do not take your holy spirit from me.
Restore to me the joy of your salvation,
and sustain in me a willing spirit.
Then I will teach transgressors your ways,
and sinners will return to you. Amen.

First Sunday in Lent

Genesis 9:8–17   1 Peter 3:18–22
Psalm 25:1–10   Mark 1:9–15

OPENING WORDS / CALL TO WORSHIP
[This may be used for each Sunday in Lent.]
From water to wilderness:
God's covenant continues;
God's kingdom comes near.

On stone and in hearts:
God's covenant continues;
God's kingdom comes near.

From the ancestor of nations to the Son lifted up:
God's covenant continues;
God's kingdom comes near.

We follow Jesus on the Lenten path,
for where he is, we would be also.   *John 12:26*
[or]
People of the covenant: *Ps. 25:10,*
God does not remember us according to our sins   *7–8, 4–5*
    and transgressions.
God remembers us according to God's own
    steadfast love!

The God of our salvation teaches us right paths and
    leads us in truth.
All the paths of the Lord are steadfast love
    and faithfulness;
we put our trust in God.

CALL TO CONFESSION

God's bow has been hung in the clouds—   *Gen. 9:13*
a unilateral disarmament in spite of our sin.
God remains faithful to the covenant of steadfast love,
even when we are unfaithful.
Without fear, then,
we confess our sins.

PRAYER OF CONFESSION

God of mercy,
we begin this Lenten season in confession.
We do not live according to your ways,
but according to our own.
We condone violence,
participate in systems of injustice,
and use power to our own advantage
at the expense of others.
Forgive us, we pray,
when we are tempted to follow paths   *Ps. 25:4*
other than those you set before us.

Teach us your commandments;
help us to turn from evil in its many guises,   *Mark 1:12*
and turn us toward your kingdom drawing near.
In covenantal love, remember us, we pray,
and be for us, once more and always,
an ark of safety and new life.
In Christ's name we pray. Amen.

DECLARATION OF FORGIVENESS

As Noah and his family were brought safely   *1 Pet. 3:20–21*
through the flood onto dry ground,
so in baptismal waters
we are brought from death into new life in Christ.
Jesus Christ, who is at the right hand of God,   *1 Pet. 3:22*
forgives us and reconciles us and all things
in heaven and on earth.
Thanks be to God for this good news!

PRAYER OF THE DAY

Loving God,
you have made covenant with us   *Gen. 9:9–11*
and with every living creature.
We give thanks for the sign of the rainbow,
for it reminds you and us of your promise:
that the flood of destruction will not be the last word.
We thank you, too, for the waters of baptism,   *Mark 1:9*
the sign that we are raised as children of the covenant;
through Jesus Christ our Lord.
And we thank you for the sign of the dove,   *Mark 1:10*
the promise of your Holy Spirit.
Hovering over the dawn of creation,   *Gen. 1:2*
descending upon your beloved Son,   *Mark 1:10*
your Spirit also
hovers over
and descends upon us.
With the whole creation,
we give you all glory and honor.
In your triune name we pray. **Amen.**

PRAYER FOR ILLUMINATION

Gracious God,
in rushing waters and in dry wilderness,   *Gen. 7:11–12;*
in every season and circumstance,   *Mark 1:12*
we need your sustaining word.
By the power of your Holy Spirit,
proclaim the good news among us today   *Mark 1:14–15*
so that we may repent and believe
and see anew how the time is fulfilled
and the kingdom has come near;
in Jesus Christ your Son, our Savior. **Amen.**

PRAYERS OF INTERCESSION

Steadfast God,
thank you for sheltering us in the storms of life.   *Gen. 7:17*
Thank you for ministering to us through angels
        seen and unseen   *Mark 1:13*
in times that test us.

Thank you for claiming us as a people beloved forever.
Because of your great love and care for us,
we trust you in our brightest joys and deepest needs.

We rejoice when dark clouds of trouble are overtaken
by the light of your presence and new possibilities,
when things settle down after a time of tossing about,
when the great storm is over,
and when the promise of resurrection life takes hold in us
with sure and certain hope.

Hear our prayers, we ask, for the deep needs of the world.
In places of violence and warfare,
give us the courage to lay down our weapons of death
and promote life and well-being instead.
In places of drought and fire,
bring rains that make the earth colorful and verdant again.
In places where the waters overtake their boundaries,
allow the overflowing chaos to recede.

Loving God,
in life and in death, we belong to you.
So in the midst of life, we entrust ourselves to your care.
We are bold to ask for help
when we are confused, lost, or afraid.
We are eager to ask for healing for our bodies and minds,
whether wounded, ill, or recovering.
And we are unceasing in our prayers for those we love
who are far from us physically, emotionally, or spiritually.
In the midst of death and grief,
even though we are weary,
we return again and again, praying for comfort,
for an easing of the pain that comes from loss,
and for the light of your presence to pierce
    the present darkness.

As the heavens were torn open at Jesus' baptism,   *Mark 1:10*
and the curtain in the temple was torn
    at his crucifixion,   *Mark 15:38*
so now tear open anything that divides us from you
or hides your presence in our lives or in the church.

We desire to hear your voice of love,
to receive the gift of the Holy Spirit,
and to see you clearly.
Lead us to serve others faithfully as disciples of Jesus Christ,
in whose name we pray. **Amen.**

INVITATION TO THE OFFERING

Because we believe that in Jesus Christ,
God's time is fulfilled and the kingdom of God
    has come near,   *Mark 1:15*
we respond in tangible ways.
By doing acts of justice and compassion
and by sharing our resources,
we bear witness to the good news of the gospel.
The offering is received in gratitude to God.

PRAYER OF THANKSGIVING/DEDICATION

God of steadfast love and faithfulness,
we are humbled as we try to do what is right   *Ps. 25:9*
and to walk in your ways.
Receive, we ask, these offerings,
and use them for your own good purposes
in the church and in all creation.
We pray in Jesus Christ. **Amen.**

CHARGE

Emerging from the waters of baptism,
Jesus became the first citizen of God's new realm.
We, who are baptized into Christ,
now live under God's rule.
In this season of Lent,
practice the way of life to which we have been called—
the way of Jesus Christ.
[or]
As Jesus spent forty days in the wilderness,   *Mark 1:13*
so we will spend forty days in this season of Lent.
Consider, children of the covenant,
the faithfulness of God,
and what it means to be baptized into Christ.
Live each day proclaiming the good news,

in word and deed,
that God is with us
and the kingdom is near.

BLESSING

May the God of covenant faithfulness enfold you;
the beloved Son encourage you;
and the Holy Spirit descend upon you in blessing;
this day and forever.

Question for Reflection

The phrase "kingdom of God" occurs fourteen times in the Gospel of Mark. Though Jesus is described at the Gospel's opening as being "from Nazareth of Galilee" (Mark 1:9), at Jesus' baptism it becomes clear whence he comes and to whom he belongs. Jesus is God's beloved Son, and his baptism signals the only realm to which he owes allegiance. His baptism, then, not only is a religious act, but also is a political and economic one. In what ways does your baptism into Christ make claims on your political, social, and economic practices as well as your religious practices?

Household Prayer: Morning

God of ancient covenants,
your steadfast love and faithfulness
are still new every morning.
I thank you that I can begin this day
in the confidence of your abiding love and unending mercy.
Help me to treat others—
family, friends,
coworkers, classmates,
and even strangers—
with love and mercy in our encounters today.
When I disappoint or am discordant,
help me to show love to others.
Open my eyes to the places, people, and circumstances
in which your kingdom has come near.
I pray in the name of your beloved Son,
Jesus Christ, my Savior. Amen.

God of peace,
as the day draws to a close
and the evening draws in around me,
I think of the creatures of the earth
that also seek rest in the hours of the night.
You love them even as you love me,
and your covenant faithfulness covers all of us.   *Gen. 9:9*
So, with the birds of the air,
the beasts of the field,
and the tiny ones who burrow in the ground,
I offer you all thanks and praise:
for your unending goodness;
for the beauty of our home, the earth;
for your gift of life instead of a deserved destruction.
As your colorful bow now rests in the clouds,   *Gen. 9:13*
so may we color the earth with the ways of peace
until all creation rests with you in completeness.   *Gen. 2:2–3*
In Christ's name I pray. Amen.

Second Sunday in Lent

Genesis 17:1–7, 15–16   Romans 4:13–25
Psalm 22:23–31   Mark 8:31–38 *or* Mark 9:2–9

OPENING WORDS / CALL TO WORSHIP
Christ died for our trespasses but was raised
   for our justification.   *Rom. 4:25*
Thanks be to God.

CALL TO CONFESSION
Trusting in God's promise of salvation,   *Rom. 4:21*
let us confess our sin and repent.

PRAYER OF CONFESSION
Merciful God,
we confess that we have not been
   sincere Christians.   *Mark 8:34–37*
We claim to follow Jesus
but have not taken his path of sacrificial love.
We profess to be disciples,
but we are not willing to bear the cost of discipleship.
We affirm the virtue of self-denial,
but we indulge our selfish desires and seek earthly gain.
Forgive us, we pray.
Free us for sincere repentance
through Jesus Christ, our Lord. Amen.

DECLARATION OF FORGIVENESS
Hear the good news: *Rom. 4:24*
God deems as righteous all who trust that Jesus
has been raised from the dead for our salvation.
In the name of Jesus Christ,
you are forgiven.
Thanks be to God.

PRAYER OF THE DAY

God, your Son Jesus Christ bore the cross
    for our salvation *Rom. 4:25*
and was raised from the dead for the redemption
    of the world.
Give us the courage to take up our cross
    and follow him, *Mark 8:34*
that through his grace we may accept
    the cost of faithful discipleship
and receive the joy of everlasting life with Christ,
who lives with you and the Holy Spirit,
one God, now and forever. **Amen.**

PRAYER FOR ILLUMINATION

Holy Spirit,
open our hearts to receive your Word,
reveal to us the good news,
and enable us to trust in the promise of salvation
in Jesus Christ. **Amen.**

PRAYERS OF INTERCESSION

Trusting in God's promises,
let us pray for the world and for our needs, saying,
Holy God, hear our prayer.

God, you blessed Abraham and Sarah *Rom. 4:13–25*
and promised to make them the ancestors
    of many nations.
In Jesus Christ you have opened your covenant
    to everyone who lives by faith in you.
For all the descendants of Abraham and Sarah,
both Jews and Christians,
that they may trust in your promise,
dwell together in peace, and be a sign of your abiding love,
Holy God, **hear our prayer.**

God, Jesus your Son called disciples to follow his way
    of sacrificial love. *Mark 8:35*
For all pastors and teachers,
that they lead the church by humble example,

take up their cross in faithful service,
and live for the sake of the gospel,
Holy God, **hear our prayer.**

God, your reign encompasses all the earth, *Ps. 22:27–28*
though many do not remember your
    gracious sovereignty.
For peace among the nations
and for integrity within governments,
that your will be done on earth as in heaven,
Holy God, **hear our prayer.**

God, you hear the cry of the poor, *Ps. 22:26*
and you satisfy the hungry with good things.
For the poor and the oppressed,
that they may find deliverance,
and for all who voluntarily take up the cross of self-denial
to serve the poor and alleviate human misery,
Holy God, **hear our prayer.**

God, you know the needs of the afflicted *Ps. 22:24*
and you hear their cries.
For those who suffer illness of mind or body,
that they may find relief from suffering
and be restored to wholeness,
Holy God, **hear our prayer.**

Grant these prayers, Holy God, by your grace.
Stir up in us the will to seek out your kingdom
with the dedication of our lives in ministry to the world,
for the sake of the gospel of Jesus Christ,
through whom we pray. **Amen.**

INVITATION TO THE OFFERING
What will it profit us to gain the whole world *Mark 8:36*
and forfeit our life?
With all humility let us make our offering to God,
trusting not in worldly gain, but in God's sustaining grace.

PRAYER OF THANKSGIVING/DEDICATION

Almighty God, we thank you for the covenant
you established with Abraham and Sarah,
which you have opened to us through Jesus Christ our Lord.
Accept these offerings with the dedication of our lives,
that we may be for the world a sign of your abiding love
and a testament to your enduring promise.
In Christ, by the power of the Holy Spirit, all honor
    and glory are yours,
Almighty God, now and forever. **Amen.**

CHARGE

Disciples of Jesus,
do not shun the way of the cross,
but follow wherever our Lord may lead.

BLESSING

May the blessing of God,
Father, Son, and Holy Spirit,
uphold you on the way.

Questions for Reflection

Jesus asks his disciples to deny themselves, take up their cross, and follow
him. How do you practice self-denial for the sake of the gospel? Is every
instance of self-denial an act of obedience to Jesus? Can some forms of self-
denial foster oppression?

Household Prayer: Morning

Lord Jesus,
help me walk with you this day.
If you lead me where I fear to go,
give me courage and keep me true,
that I may bear my cross without shame
and live in the promise of life eternal. Amen.

Household Prayer: Evening

Jesus, if I stray,
show me my fault,
forgive my sin,
and set me rightly on your path.
Keep me on the way of the cross,
and lead me to the eternal joy of Easter. Amen.

Third Sunday in Lent

Exodus 20:1–17   1 Corinthians 1:18–25
Psalm 19   John 2:13–22

OPENING WORDS / CALL TO WORSHIP
Heaven is declaring God's glory;   *Ps. 19:1–4*
the sky is proclaiming God's handiwork.
One day gushes the news to the next,
and one night informs another what needs to be known.
There is no speech; there are no words;
their voices cannot be heard by us.
Yet their sound extends throughout the world;
their words reach the ends of the earth!
[or]
[May be read antiphonally]
The law of the Lord is perfect,   *Ps. 19:7–11*
reviving the soul;
the decrees of the Lord are sure,
making wise the simple;
the precepts of the Lord are right,
rejoicing the heart;
the commandment of the Lord is clear,
enlightening the eyes;
the fear of the Lord is pure,
enduring forever;
the ordinances of the Lord are true
and righteous altogether.
**They are more desirable than gold, and sweeter
    than honey.**
In keeping them is great reward.
[or]

The message of the cross sounds foolish
to the world;   *1 Cor. 1:18, 23–25*
But to us it is the power of God!
We proclaim the scandal of Christ crucified.
The foolishness of God is wiser than human wisdom,
and the weakness of God is stronger than our strength.

CALL TO CONFESSION
Despite all that God has taught us,
we still act foolishly;
we are still weak.
In the cross of Christ,
we find forgiveness and grace.
We confess our sins,
trusting in God's wisdom and strength
rather than our own.

PRAYER OF CONFESSION
Merciful God,
how fickle we are; we sin against you
without even knowing it.   *Ps. 19:12–13*
Clear us, we pray, of any unknown sin,
and save us from willfully ignoring your way.
Let your commandments rule and guide us.

Forgive us for worshiping anyone or anything
except you;   *Exod. 20:4–5*
keep us faithful.

Forgive us for failing to honor all
our relationships—   *Exod. 20:12, 14*
with those closest to us and those
who are distant neighbors.
Help us to speak words of blessing
and kindness,
rather than words that belittle or destroy.
Turn us away from violence, falsehood,
and selfishness.   *Exod. 20:12–17*

Forgive us for thinking everything depends
    on our efforts and power,
for you are the God who made us,
    led us out slavery,   *Exod. 20:2, 8–11*
and has brought us into the community of faith.
Help us to depend on you alone
and to rest in your peace.
In Christ's name we pray. Amen.

DECLARATION OF FORGIVENESS

Brothers and sisters,
in Jesus Christ, crucified, risen, and coming again,
we are forgiven and set free to live in faithfulness
with God and with one another!
Thanks be to God!

READING OF THE TEN COMMANDMENTS

*[The Law may also be read before the prayer
of confession.]*
I am the Lord your God,   *Exod. 20:2–17*
who brought you out of the land of Egypt,
out of the house of slavery;
you shall have no other gods before me.
You shall not make for yourself an idol.
You shall not make wrongful use of the name
    of the Lord your God.
Remember the sabbath day, and keep it holy.
Honor your father and your mother.
You shall not murder.
You shall not commit adultery.
You shall not steal.
You shall not bear false witness against your neighbor.
You shall not covet your neighbor's house;
you shall not covet your neighbor's wife,
or male or female slave,
or ox, or donkey, or anything that belongs
    to your neighbor.
[or]
Brothers and sisters in Christ,
as forgiven people,

we are now freed to live in grateful response to God,
following God's law, which is our guide for
　　full and abundant life:

We are freed to worship God and God alone . . .
freed from having to make anything an idol.

We are freed to call on the name of the Lord without
　　abusing God's name.

We are freed for a day of worship and rest,
freed to love those who gave us birth and nurtured us.

Freed from all that binds us,
　　we shall not kill or break sacred bonds;
　　we need not steal or lie,
　　nor crave anything that belongs to another.

God's law brings us goodness and blessing;
God's grace gives us confidence and joy.

PRAYER OF THE DAY

Gracious God,
whose power is made perfect in weakness,   *2 Cor. 12:9*
whose wisdom appears as foolishness in this world,   *1 Cor. 1:25*
we thank you for the scandal of the cross.
In Jesus Christ,
you overturn all our usual ways of behaving
　　and believing.   *John 2:15–21*
You scatter our false notions of discipleship
as easily as coins are spilled from a box.
You correct our notions of piety and order
　　with fierce passion.
Do not let your church become content or
　　contained as an institution.
Raze to ruins what is distorted in us,
and raise us to new life as a community
so that we may be the body of Christ in and for the world.
With fear and joy we ask this in Christ's name. **Amen.**

PRAYER FOR ILLUMINATION

God of Glory,
we cannot hear the heavens proclaim
    your handiwork,   *Ps. 19:1–4*
though the speech of the skies must
    be magnificent.
We cannot hear what day and night are
    singing about you,
though their song must be both bright
    and deep.
Yet, somehow you are made known to us   *1 Cor. 1:21*
through our own foolish proclamation.
It is only by the power of the Holy Spirit
that your Word can be heard in our words.
Open our ears to what you are saying to us today,
    we pray;
and perhaps we may also hear echoes
    of your glory
in the broad firmament above.
In Christ's name we pray. **Amen.**

[or]

Holy Spirit of God,
let the words of my mouth   *Ps. 19:14*
and the mediations of our hearts
be acceptable in your sight,
O Lord, our rock and our redeemer. **Amen.**

PRAYERS OF INTERCESSION

Holy God,
you have called us to live before you
and with one another
in all faithfulness.
Unable to live as you intend,
we inflict harm and hurt on others
and on ourselves as well.
In all these ways,
we know we grieve your heart also.
Hear, then, our prayers of intercession.

Restore us to communion with you and one another
that we might live in the freedom you have bestowed.

We pray for people who are victims of crime,   *Exod. 20:13, 15*
from petty theft to murder.
We pray that those harmed will find healing
and will dwell in safety.
Hold especially close to your heart, O God,
those who have lost a loved one to violence;
and help us to offer tenderness and care
in their struggles and grief.
We pray also for those who have committed crimes,
that they may seek and find forgiveness,
and begin a new life of responsibility and integrity
before you and in the community.

We pray for healing and reconciliation where trust
      has been broken,   *Exod. 20:12,*
hostility has flared, or misunderstanding has grown.   *14, 16–17*
Restore us not only to one another,
but reconcile us to ourselves and to you, loving God.
If restoration proves beyond hope,
then grant new beginnings and possibilities for all.
In every relationship, we seek your grace as we
      honor others
by caring for them,
being truthful,
and working for their welfare.
Root out in us any jealousy toward what others possess,
and let generosity grow in and among us instead.

Gracious God,
we pray for those who are ill, in mind, body, or spirit;
for those lonely and isolated from community;
for those burdened by guilt or grief,
by depression or despair.
Do not let us turn inward as a church,
lest we shut out or neglect
those who long for a community of welcome
      and companionship.

Send us out in love, with open eyes, ears, and hearts.
Make us true neighbors to one another
and true children of your own calling.
We pray in the name of Christ,
who has come to set us free. **Amen.**   *Gal. 5:1*

INVITATION TO THE OFFERING

The house of God is not a marketplace for
    buying and selling.   *John 2:16*
It is a house of prayer,
a place of healing and restoration,
a place where we bring before God our provisions
to be used for present needs.
Let us bring our tithes and offerings to God.

PRAYER OF THANKSGIVING/DEDICATION

O Lord our God,
we want to follow all your commandments—
to love only you, not worshiping the things
    of this world;   *Exod. 20:2–4*
to love our neighbor freely,   *Exod. 20:17*
not desiring for ourselves something they possess.
Accept these offerings, we pray,
and teach us to be generous,
giving fully of ourselves
that we may truly be the body of Christ in this world. **Amen.**

CHARGE

In the Lenten week ahead,
study God's commandments,   *Exod. 20:1–17*
practice the way of life they teach,
and see how God's laws revive your soul.   *Ps. 19:7–8, 11*
[or]
In the Lenten week ahead,
find time and space to listen for God's glory   *Ps. 19:1–4*
as it is spoken in the world around you.

BLESSING

> May God shine upon you,
> Christ fill you with true wisdom and strength,
> and the Holy Spirit guide you into all faithfulness,
> now and forever.

Question for Reflection

The third Sunday of Lent focuses on the gift of God's law (Exod. 20:1–17). John Calvin (1509–1564) described three uses for the Ten Commandments: First, they show us how to live before God and neighbor, and expose our sins in failing to live as God intends. Second, they instruct our civic or common life, showing us how to live responsibly in the freedom God gives. Third, rather than show us what we must do in order to *receive* God's grace and love, the commandments show us how we should live *because* we are a people who have already received God's grace and love in Jesus Christ. Does God's law restrict or enhance our freedom as human beings?

Household Prayer: Morning

God of heaven and earth,
I listen this morning for the sound of your glory:
in the songs of birds,
in quiet conversations that begin the day,
in easy laughter among friends,
in sunlight's warmth,
pattering rain, or silent snowfall.
Give me ears to hear your glory in its many forms.
Give me eyes to see your glory in its many guises.
Throughout this day, I, too, will proclaim your glory,
your grace, and your love
so that I may be a part of the chorus of praise
that stretches to the ends of the earth.
In Christ's name I pray. Amen.

Household Prayer: Evening

God of freedom,
I thank you for claiming me as your own
and for setting me in the midst of the community of faith.
Today the news was filled with stories of people
who do not live according to your commandments,
with grievous results.
Lives are shattered
as your ancient tablets of stone are broken again and again.
And I struggle, too, in my own ways,
to live before you and my neighbors
in faithfulness, generosity, and love.
As the day comes to an end,
I pray for forgiveness for myself
and for this weary world,
confident of your grace and mercy.
Send your gift of Sabbath rest,
and let me sleep in peace as, over and around me,
night declares to night your power and glory.
In Jesus' name I pray. Amen.

Fourth Sunday in Lent

Numbers 21:4–9   Ephesians 2:1–10
Psalm 107:1–3, 17–22   John 3:14–21

OPENING WORDS / CALL TO WORSHIP
O give thanks to the Lord, who is good;   *Ps. 107:1*
God's steadfast love endures forever.

CALL TO CONFESSION
This is the judgment, that the light has
   come into the world,   *John 3:19*
for people loved darkness rather than light
   because their deeds were evil.
Let us uncover our sin before the liberating
   light of Christ.

PRAYER OF CONFESSION
Merciful God,   *Num. 21:4–6*
we confess the folly of our sin and the hypocrisy
   of our complaints.
We grumble about the evils in our world,
even as we commit injustices and profit through deceit.
We fret about the scarcity of resources
while hoarding earth's goods and cheating the poor.
We protest the problems of our world,
but we do not actively work to address them.
Merciful God, expose our sins before the light of your grace.
Heal our sin and free us from our foolish ways
that we me know the joy of eternal life in Jesus Christ,
in whose name we pray. Amen.

DECLARATION OF FORGIVENESS

Indeed, God did not send the Son into the world
 to condemn the world, *John 3:17*
but in order that the world might be saved through him.
In the name of Jesus Christ, you are forgiven.
Thanks be to God.

PRAYER OF THE DAY

Almighty God, through Jesus Christ you bring
 salvation to the world. *Eph. 2:10*
Give us strength to believe in him
that we may share in his victory over the power of death
and fulfill the purpose for which you have made us,
for he dwells with you and the Holy Spirit,
one God, forever and ever. **Amen.**

PRAYER FOR ILLUMINATION

Almighty God, *John 3:21*
by the power of the Holy Spirit,
open your Word and illumine our darkened world,
that we may see clearly and live faithfully
by the light of your truth in Jesus Christ. **Amen.**

PRAYERS OF INTERCESSION

Sisters and brothers,
confident in God's love and mercy,
let us pray for the world and for our needs, saying,
Merciful God, hear our prayer.

Holy God, you created us in Christ Jesus
 for good works. *Eph. 2:10*
Help those who profess faith in Christ to do good
 in the world,
following the way of life you have prepared
 for those who believe in him.
For the church of Jesus Christ,
Merciful God, **hear our prayer.**

Your children walk by your light, doing what is true.   *Eph. 2:8–9*
Yet salvation is not earned by good works,
but through trust in your grace.
Dispel from your children arrogance of heart,
that the world may be drawn to your truth
by their humble witness.
Merciful God, **hear our prayer.**

In every age you call forth men and women of integrity
to lead your people in the way of righteousness.
Help pastors and teachers fulfill their calling;
give them courage to speak the truth in love,
and shield them from temptation to misuse their authority.
For pastors and teachers,
Merciful God, **hear our prayer.**

God, your reign encompasses all the earth,   *Eph. 2:1–3*
though the nations may rebel against your justice.
Save the nations from the wrath of their disobedience.
Help them to dwell in peace and promote the
     common good.
For governments and leaders,
Merciful God, **hear our prayer.**

You hear the cry of the sick and the afflicted.   *Ps. 107:17–20*
Save them from their distress,
heal them of their disease,
and deliver them from the destructive power
     of suffering.
For all who sorrow in distress,
Merciful God, **hear our prayer.**

O God, in Jesus Christ   *John 3:16*
you have shown your love for the world.
Receive our prayers, grant us what we need,
save us from perishing, and bring us to everlasting life.
     Amen.

INVITATION TO THE OFFERING

People of God, let us offer our sacrifice of thanksgiving,   *Ps. 107:21*
telling of God's deeds with songs of joy.

PRAYER OF THANKSGIVING/DEDICATION

Merciful God, we thank you for your
    wonderful works among humankind.   *Ps. 107:22*
Accept this offering with the dedication
    of our lives
and help us be for the world an emblem
    of your steadfast love,   *Ps. 107:1*
in Jesus Christ. **Amen.**

CHARGE

Church, we have received the immeasurable riches
    of God's grace   *Eph. 2:7*
in kindness toward us in Christ Jesus.
Go forth to share this gift with others.

BLESSING

May the love of God,
the grace of Christ,
and the light of the Spirit
bless you and keep you in the way of truth.

Questions for Reflection

What does the light of God's truth reveal about your life? Are there parts of
your life that you want to hide from God? Can you imagine what it would
be like to live completely transparent to God's piercing light?

Household Prayer: Morning

Loving God,
draw me to your light,
that I may avoid the dangers of sin
and receive the freedom of your grace
in Jesus Christ. Amen.

Household Prayer: Evening

Lord Christ,
as shadows of night draw near,
sustain me by the light that banishes the fearful claim of death.
Help me believe in you with all my heart
that I may know the freedom of salvation
and at last receive the joy of eternal life. Amen.

Fifth Sunday in Lent

Jeremiah 31:31–34   Hebrews 5:5–10
Psalm 51:1–12 *or* Psalm 119:9–16   John 12:20–33

OPENING WORDS / CALL TO WORSHIP

Jesus said, "When I am lifted up, I will draw all people
     to myself."   *John 12:32*
Blessed be the God of our salvation
who bears our burdens and forgives our sins.

CALL TO CONFESSION

Let us pray for the cleansing of our hearts,   *Ps. 51:10*
confessing our sins to the One whose mercy
     is everlasting.

PRAYER OF CONFESSION

Redeeming God,
we confess that we have not loved you
     with our whole heart,
and have not loved our neighbors as we ought;
we have strayed from your commandments.   *Ps. 119:10*
Do not remember our sins, but forgive
     our iniquities,   *Jer. 31:34*
that we may fix our eyes on you and sin no more,   *Ps. 119:15b*
through Christ our Lord. Amen.

DECLARATION OF FORGIVENESS

Sisters and brothers, by the faith of Christ,
your sins are forgiven.
May you delight in the joy of your salvation.

PRAYER OF THE DAY

Holy God, by the cross and resurrection
    of Jesus,   *Jer. 31:33; John 12:32*
you lift the suffering world toward hope
    and transformation
and open the way to eternal salvation.
As we move ever closer to the passion of Christ,
may your law of love be written on our hearts
as he draws all people to himself revealing
    your love for the world. **Amen.**

PRAYER FOR ILLUMINATION

Your Word, O God, has power to
    change our lives   *Ps. 119:10–11, 15*
and to create a whole new world.
As we meditate on your word this day,
fill us with your Holy Spirit,
that we may treasure your word with
    our whole hearts
and fix our eyes on you. **Amen.**

PRAYERS OF INTERCESSION

[Optional response after each petition:]
Create in us a clean heart, O God,
and renew a right spirit within us.

During the final days of his earthly life,   *Heb. 5:7, 9*
Jesus offered up prayers and supplications with
    loud cries and tears,
and in faithful obedience, he opened the way
    to eternal salvation.
Let us open our hearts this day as we lift up
    our deepest needs and concerns
to the One who is mighty to save.

We pray for all leaders and people,
that by the power of your cross
you would drive out all violence, domination,
    and injustice in our world
as you draw us to your Christ.

We pray for our war-ravaged world,
that you would teach us to walk together
in your way of righteousness and peace.

We pray for the vocation of the church,
that our prayers would bear the fruit of action
as we hear the cries of pain and suffering of those in need.

We pray for the poor, the terrified, and the oppressed,
and those who are too much alone,
that they may find a home in you as we serve them
in your name.

As your son anticipated his death on the cross
in light of your steadfast love,
may all who have died or who are dying be at rest
in your eternal care.

Through Christ, with Christ,
in the unity of the Holy Spirit,
we glorify you, almighty God,
with unending thanks and praise. **Amen.**

INVITATION TO THE OFFERING
Unless a grain of wheat falls to the ground   *John 12:24*
and takes on new life, it remains just a single grain.
With grateful hearts,
let us bring the fruit of our lives to God.

PRAYER OF THANKSGIVING/DEDICATION
As the high priest Melchizedek blessed Abraham   *Gen. 14:18*
and offered his tithe of bread and wine
at your holy altar,
may our gifts be made perfect through Christ   *Heb. 5:5, 6, 9*
to glorify you and bless the world. **Amen.**

CHARGE
Jesus said, "Whoever serves me must follow me,   *John 12:26*
and where I am, there will my servant be also."
Go in peace to love and serve Christ.

BLESSING

May God, whose hand has written the law of love
    upon your heart,   *Jer. 31:33*
fill you with peace from deep within
and the commitment to live in harmony.
And the blessing of God, who loves, forgives,
    and calls us home,
be with you now and always.

Questions for Reflection

God is at work offering forgiveness, showing mercy, and giving knowledge of life, death, and salvation. Where is God enacting that new life within or around you? What in your life must die so that you may flourish? What must fall away so that you can rise again in Christ?

Household Prayer: Morning

Loving God, you offer the gift of new life each day.
Open my heart to receive this grace that I may be wholly yours,
then give me the courage to share this gift wherever I go
as I seek to walk in your way of mercy, forgiveness, and newness of life.
Amen.

Household Prayer: Evening

Forgiving God, who makes all things new,
you know where I have flourished this day,
and you know where I have failed.
Help me to know that in all my challenges there is a seed of hope
that enables me to more faithfully depend on you.
May I rest in peace this night and awake refreshed
to greet the newness of your day. Amen.

Palm Sunday / Passion Sunday

LITURGY OF THE PALMS

Psalm 118:1–2, 19–29   Mark 11:1–11
                              or John 12:12–16

LITURGY OF THE PASSION

Isaiah 50:4–9a   Philippians 2:5–11
Psalm 31:9–16   Mark 14:1–15:47
                    or Mark 15:1–39 (40–47)

OPENING WORDS / CALL TO WORSHIP

Blessed is the coming kingdom.
Hosanna in the highest!

When Jesus and his disciples were approaching
    Jerusalem,   *Mark 11:1–6*
at Bethphage and Bethany, near the Mount of Olives,
    he sent two of his disciples
and said to them, "Go into the village ahead of you,
    and immediately as you enter it,
you will find tied there a colt that has never been ridden;
    untie it and bring it.
If anyone says to you, 'Why are you doing this?'
    just say this,
'The Lord needs it and will send it back here
    immediately.'"
They went away and found a colt tied near a door,
    outside in the street.
As they were untying it, some of the bystanders
    said to them,
"What are you doing, untying the colt?"
They told them what Jesus had said; and they allowed
    them to take it.

Blessed is the coming kingdom.
Hosanna in the highest!

Then they brought the colt to Jesus and threw
    their cloaks on it;   *Mark 11:7–11*
and he sat on it. Many people spread their cloaks
    on the road,
and others spread leafy branches that they had cut
    in the fields.
Then those who went ahead and those who followed
    were shouting,
"Hosanna! Blessed is the One who comes in the
    name of the Lord!
Blessed is the coming kingdom of our ancestor David!
    Hosanna in the highest!"
Then he entered Jerusalem and went into the temple;
    and when he had looked around at everything, as it
    was already late, he went out to Bethany with the twelve.

Blessed is the coming kingdom.
Hosanna in the highest!

CALL TO CONFESSION

Let us confess our sins to God, whose steadfast love
    endures forever.   *Ps. 118:2*

PRAYER OF CONFESSION

We confess that we have sinned,
and although we would like to deny it,
we have forsaken you.
We are horrified by the suffering we cause—
to you, ourselves, and the world you have created.
Open the gates of your forgiveness and restore us
    in your love,
for the sake of our Savior, Jesus Christ. Amen.

DECLARATION OF FORGIVENESS

The Lord God helps us; we will not be disgraced.   *Isa. 50:7–9*
The Lord God helps us; who can declare us guilty?
Sister and brothers, beyond the shadow of doubt,
    your sins are forgiven.
By the mercy of Christ, let us stand together
    forgiven and free.

PRAYER OF THE DAY

God of salvation, our Lord entered his passion to raise us to life.
In this holiest of weeks, help us to walk the way of the cross,
that we may be raised in a resurrection like his
and dwell forever in you, Eternal God,
Father, Son, and Holy Spirit. **Amen.**

PRAYER FOR ILLUMINATION

Come Holy Spirit, source of all life.
As we hear again the story of the passion,
let the same mind be in us that was in Christ, *Phil. 2:5*
who was a servant that we might be free.
Awaken our ears, open our hearts, *Isa. 50:4, 5*
and sustain the weary with your Word. **Amen.**

PRAYERS OF INTERCESSION

Jesus suffered death and rose to glory for the life
    of the world.
Let us lift up our hearts in thanks to God and pray
    for the cares of the world, saying,
Save us, O Lord, for your mercy is great.

Holy God, your son humbled himself, even to death,
to show us the power of loving service.
Guide those holding positions of power,
that their decisions give rise to the mutual flourishing
    of the world you so love.
Save us, O Lord, **for your mercy is great.**

Healing God, your son is betrayed and crucified
in our violent world each day.
Raise us to a new and rightly ordered world
through the reconciling love of Christ,
where all victims of violence, persecution,
shame, or terror may stand together with you in peace.
Save us, O Lord, **for your mercy is great.**

Forsaken God, as your son suffered his cruel death
on the cross,
darkness covered the whole land.

Enlighten us to care for your creation,
awaken us from our denial and abuse,
and help us to alleviate its suffering.
Save us, O Lord, **for your mercy is great.**

Grieving God, your son consoled others in life and in death.
We pray for all who are distressed, broken, or sorrowful,
that together with Christ in his suffering
we may be healed and raised in you.
Save us, O Lord, **for your mercy is great.**

Eternal God, your son was lovingly cared for
as he was laid to rest in a tomb.
We remember before you those who have died
and pray for those who will die today;
enfold them in your love,
that they may rest and rise with Christ forever in his light.
Save us, O Lord, **for your mercy is great.**

We ask all this in the name of Jesus,
who lives and reigns with you and the Holy Spirit,
one God, now and forever. **Amen.**

INVITATION TO THE OFFERING

Jesus gave himself for the life of the world.
With humble hearts bowed in awe,
let us offer ourselves and our gifts to God.

PRAYER OF THANKSGIVING/DEDICATION

Holy God, we give thanks for your saving love
made known to us in the life, death, and resurrection of Christ.
Bless these gifts that they may bring life
on earth as in heaven;
in Christ's name we pray. **Amen.**

CHARGE

Let the same mind be in you that was in Jesus Christ. *Phil. 2:5*
Go forth in peace to love and serve the world.

BLESSING

May the blessing of God,
who surmounts evil,
bears our pain,
and lives in us forever,
fill you with a zeal for justice
and passion for peace,
this day and always.

Questions for Reflection

The passion of Christ is a story of terror in which, against all odds, love wins. How might this story reshape your week, your life, our world? Where will you commit to letting love win? How will this change your life?

Household Prayer: Morning

Jesus, in your passion and resurrection,
you show me there is no place you have not been
and no place you fear to go.
Morning by morning, you awaken me more deeply to this truth.
Send me into the world this day with the courage and wisdom
to be a faithful witness to your coming reign
of justice, mercy, and peace. Amen.

Household Prayer: Evening

Although I have sought to serve you this day,
I have failed to keep your love.
You know my strengths and weaknesses more than I;
reveal them to me that I may be healed this night
and begin afresh tomorrow. Amen.

Holy Thursday

Exodus 12:1–4 (5–10), 11–14   1 Corinthians 11:23–26
Psalm 116:1–2, 12–19   John 13:1–17, 31b–35

OPENING WORDS / CALL TO WORSHIP
This is a day of remembrance for us.   *Exod. 12:14*
We lift up the cup of salvation   *Ps. 116:13*
and call on the name of the Lord.
Throughout the generations,   *Exod. 12:14c*
we have received and handed on to others   *1 Cor. 11:23*
what the Lord has given to us:
water for washing; the towel of service;   *John 13:4–5*
the bread of his body; the cup of the new covenant;   *1 Cor. 11:24–26*
proclaiming the Lord's death until he comes again.
[or]
[Members of the congregation bring forward a towel,
a bowl of water, a loaf of bread, and a cup of wine.]
In the growing darkness we gather.
Our Lenten journey has brought us here.
Jesus, our Teacher and Lord, sets before us   *John 13:13*
a towel,
a bowl,
bread,
a cup.
He gives us an example
and a commandment ever new: *John 13:34–35*
to love one another as he has loved us.
This is how everyone will know
we are his disciples,
when we love each other.

CALL TO CONFESSION

John 13:10–11

Even among Jesus' closest disciples,
not all were clean.
On this night of all nights,
we confess the ways we disappoint,
deny, and even betray
Jesus, our Teacher and Lord.
Our confession of sin is made in the sure knowledge
that Jesus is able to wash us in forgiveness and love.

PRAYER OF CONFESSION

Holy God,
you have called us to serve others as Christ
has served us. John 13:14–15
We confess that we have not followed
Christ's example
as fully or as often as we should.
We turn away from people in need.
True humility eludes us,
and we hide our own vulnerability before others.
You have commanded us to love one another
as you have loved us. John 13:34
We confess that we do not love so generously.
Gathered on this Holy Thursday,
we confess that we are capable of denying
and betraying you
and one another, John 13:2, 10–11
no less than the first disciples.
Forgive us, merciful God,
and cleanse us of all our sin;
then guide our feet to walk with you always.
In Christ's name we pray. Amen.

DECLARATION OF FORGIVENESS

Disciples of Christ,
having loved his own who were in the world,
Jesus loved them to the end.
Jesus knows us fully
and offers love and forgiveness unconditionally.
In gratitude for the grace given to us,

and as a witness to our faith in Christ,
we will love one another.
*[On Holy Thursday, it is especially fitting to follow the Confession of Sin
and Declaration of Forgiveness by passing the peace of Christ.]*
The peace of Christ be with you.
And also with you.

PRAYER OF THE DAY

God of love,
during Holy Week,
we give you thanks for this night
Jesus shared with his disciples.
Between the public parade
and the public charade
is this intimate hour.
Though even now we do not fully understand,   *John 13:7*
we long to follow his example:
to serve as he served,   *John 13:14, 34*
to love as he loved.
Jesus promised
that if we know these things and do them,   *John 13:17*
we will be blessed.
Help us, then, to know and to do
all that Jesus taught.
Though we betray and deny,
we still come seeking a blessing,
for this much we do know:
we cannot live unless you bless us. **Amen.**   *Gen. 32:26*

PRAYER FOR ILLUMINATION

Gracious God,
pour out your Holy Spirit upon us, we pray,
that we may see the light of your Word
in the darkness of our lives.
And seeing, may we understand;
understanding, may we do all that you ask.   *John 13:17*
In the name of Jesus Christ. **Amen.**

PRAYER FOR THE BLESSING OF WATER FOR WASHING

[If the service is to include footwashing, this prayer
may precede that act.]
Loving God,
as Jesus took a basin and poured the water long ago, *John 13:5*
we bring these basins of water before you.
Bless this water for washing,
and bless the feet of your servants, too.
Wash away the stains and strains of this life, we pray,
that we may walk anew in the ways of Christ.
In true humility, we bend our lives in service to you.
Help us all, by your example, to understand more deeply *John 13:7*
how we are meant to serve
rather than be served,
for love's sake.
In Christ we pray. **Amen.**

PRAYERS OF INTERCESSION

God of power and might,
on the night of Passover, *Exod. 12:11*
you commanded your people
to be ready to go in a hurry:
to be dressed, with sandals on their feet,
and walking stick in hand
as they ate a special meal.
We pray for people everywhere who long for freedom,
who are ready, eager to do as you have commanded.
Bring down oppression's rule;
overturn unjust laws;
break the chains of those still enslaved;
banish every form of human trafficking.
Compel us, without delay, to enter a new place
where all lives are honored and all voices are heard.

God of tenderness and compassion,
on the night before he died,
Jesus set a table for his disciples.
They took off their sandals *John 13:2b–5*
and sat down in the presence of their
   Teacher and Lord,

who washed their feet, one by one.
We pray for people whose feet are tired
    and dusty from hard labor;
for those whose backs are bent by care and worry;
for those laid low by illness or guilt or grief.
Wash away, we pray,
the tiredness of our bodies and souls.
Hold gently in your healing hands
the broken places in our lives and relationships.
Be our company in isolation,
our source of hope in despair,
and the way forward at every dead end.

God of all good gifts,
thank you for setting a table of welcome
    for everyone;
for making room whether we are faithful
    or faithless or failures.
We pray that all who are hungry will find enough to eat
and clean water to drink
as we share and live more responsibly.
Teach us to sit down with enemies,
sharing common meals and common hopes.
Make us true servants of yours for the sake
    of the world.
Teach us to love as you love for the sake
    of the world.
We pray for faith that is worth handing on to
    yet another generation   *1 Cor. 11:23*
for the sake of the world you love.
In Christ's name we pray. **Amen.**

INVITATION TO THE OFFERING
The psalmist asks,   *Ps. 116:12–14, 17–19*
What shall I return to the Lord for all God's
    bounty to me?
And then declares:
I will lift up the cup of salvation
and call on the name of the Lord;

I will pay my vows
and offer thanksgiving
in the presence of the congregation.
With gratitude for God's bounty to us,
we join the psalmist,
praising God with our offerings.

PRAYER OF THANKSGIVING/DEDICATION

We are your servants, O God,   *Ps. 116:16; Exod. 12:14*
for you have loosed all other bonds
that held us captive.
In freedom, we follow you.
In gratitude, we praise you.
Celebrating all that you have done for us in Christ,
we bring before you tithes and offerings,
bread and wine,
asking you to add your blessing
so that all that we have and all that we are
may be used in blessing others.
In Christ's name we pray. **Amen.**

CHARGE

Jesus has set an example for us: *John 13:15–16, 34–35*
to serve others as he has served us,
and to love one another as he has loved us.
Go and do likewise
so that everyone can tell
that we are his disciples.

BLESSING

May God, who led Israel out of slavery into freedom,
may Christ, who led us out of death into life,
and may the Holy Spirit, who leads us out of fear into boldness,
abide with you this Holy Thursday,
in the holy days ahead,
and forevermore.

Questions for Reflection

For Jewish people, Passover is a day of remembrance and celebration. For Christians, every Lord's Supper is also a day of remembrance and celebration. Both Jews and Christians are enjoined to hand on to the next generation what we have received from the Lord. When do you first remember receiving the Lord's Supper? What words, phrases, memories, or practices of this sacrament do you especially wish to pass on to the next generation?

Household Prayer: Morning

Each day, O Lord,
I wash my feet, my hands, and head
almost without thinking.
It is a routine of the morning,
ordinary, even perfunctory.
This morning, make me newly aware
of the water that pours out and over,
spilling in abundance,
washing me clean.
As I go through this day,
place before me an opportunity to serve someone—
family member, friend, neighbor, or stranger.
Help me bend to another's need
without seeking gain or advantage.
And, if someone should offer to serve me in some way,
give me a heart open and vulnerable enough
to receive what is offered in kindness,
all for love's sake,
which is for your sake. Amen.

Household Prayer: Evening

God of love,
thank you for knowing us fully
and loving us to the end.
On this night of the Christian year especially,
I am grateful to be part of the community of Jesus' disciples.

Thank you for all those who handed the faith on to me,
and those who continue to teach me by example
what it means to serve you
and to serve one another.
Thank you for making a place for me at your table,
even though I fall short
of what you have called me to be and to do.
In evening's rest,
I remember that, for Jesus, no rest would come
this night or tomorrow.
Yet, in forgiveness and love,
he is with us always:
the light shining in the darkness. Amen.

Good Friday

Isaiah 52:13–53:12   Hebrews 10:16–25 *or*
Psalm 22   Hebrews 4:14–16; 5:7–9
                       John 18:1–19:42

OPENING WORDS / CALL TO WORSHIP

We enter into a holy place   *Ps. 22:9–10; Heb. 10:19–20*
through the new and living way
Jesus Christ has opened for us.
We come as a holy people—
born of the grace of Jesus Christ,
delivered through his blood.

CALL TO CONFESSION

[Pouring water into the font]
In Christ, we have a great high priest   *Heb. 4:14–16*
who knows our every weakness.
He has been tested as we are,
yet his faithfulness never failed.

Therefore, we dare to approach the throne of grace,
trusting God's mercy as we confess our sin.

PRAYER OF CONFESSION

*[Alternately, the Solemn Reproaches of the Cross
may be used; see below.]*
Lord Jesus Christ, we confess to you: *Isa. 53:6–7;*
like sheep, we all go astray.   *John 18:1–19:42*
Lamb of God, have mercy on us.

We betray you; we deny you;
like sheep, we all go astray.
Lamb of God, have mercy on us.

We mock you; we scorn you;
like sheep, we all go astray.
Lamb of God, have mercy on us.

We abandon you; we forsake you;
like sheep, we all go astray.
Lamb of God, have mercy on us.

We condemn you; we crucify you;
like sheep, we all go astray.
Lamb of God, have mercy on us.

Lamb of God, have mercy on us,
**and by your grace, Lord Jesus Christ,
save us from our sin. Amen.**

DECLARATION OF FORGIVENESS
[Lifting water from the font]
Let us live in the full assurance of our faith,   *Heb. 10:22*
with our hearts cleansed of all evil
and our bodies washed with living water.

This is the good news of Good Friday:
In Jesus Christ we are forgiven.
Thanks be to God.

PRAYER OF THE DAY
We stand near the cross, O God—   *John 19:25–27, 31*
disturbed, distraught, discouraged.
Yet we gather here as disciples,
those whom Jesus loves.
On this day of great solemnity,
let us stand as witnesses
to your great love for all the world,
revealed in the outstretched arms
of Jesus Christ our Lord. **Amen.**

PRAYER FOR ILLUMINATION
In the darkness of this hour,   *Isa. 53:11*
Lord, be our light.

By the breath of your Spirit,
whisper the Word of life
that death cannot destroy:
Jesus Christ our Savior. **Amen.**

PRAYERS OF INTERCESSION
*[Alternately, the Solemn Intercession of Good Friday
may be used; see below.]*
In the days of his flesh, *Isa. 52:13; Ps. 22:19;*
Jesus offered his prayers *Heb. 5:7–9*
with loud cries and tears
to the One who was able
to save him from death.

On this day, we pray in Jesus' name:
O Lord, do not be far away;
O God, come quickly to help us.

Remember your church. . . .
Keep us faithful to the gospel,
proclaiming the good news of salvation
even in the face of danger and death.
O Lord, do not be far away;
O God, come quickly to help us.

Remember your world. . . .
Rescue this perishing planet,
condemned by human cruelty;
do not let it be destroyed forever.
O Lord, do not be far away;
O God, come quickly to help us.

Remember all nations. . . .
Break the sword and snap the spear;
trample the high walls and thorny fences
that separate neighbors and nations.
O Lord, do not be far away;
O God, come quickly to help us.

Remember those who face death. . . .
Restore the lives of those who suffer,
give hope to those who are despairing,
and welcome the dying into your arms.
O Lord, do not be far away;
O God, come quickly to help us.

We ask these things in the name of Jesus,
your suffering servant,
our only hope of salvation. **Amen.**

INVITATION TO THE OFFERING
Let us provoke one another   *Heb. 10:24*
to love and good deeds,
giving our lives for one another
in the name of the One
who gave his life for us.

PRAYER OF THANKSGIVING/DEDICATION
We give you thanks and praise, O God,   *Ps. 22:14; John 19:28*
that you have poured out your love for us
through the life and death of Jesus Christ.
Teach us to pour out our love for others,
sharing your deep goodness and grace
with a world that is thirsty for new life;
in the name of Jesus Christ our Lord. **Amen.**

CHARGE
Hold fast to your hope,   *Heb. 10:23*
for God is faithful. **Amen.**

BLESSING
*[All may depart in silence after the closing hymn. Good Friday is
understood to be one movement in a three-day service (the* Triduum, *or
"Three Days"), spanning Holy Thursday, Good Friday, and the Great Vigil
of Easter. Traditionally, the blessing is omitted on Good Friday, since the
service continues at the Easter Vigil or on Easter Sunday.]*

SOLEMN REPROACHES OF THE CROSS

[This brief litany is modeled after the Solemn Reproaches of the Cross, a Good Friday tradition that can be traced to the Middle Ages. Here the Solemn Reproaches are streamlined and simplified for contemporary worship.]

The cross that held the Savior of the world.
Holy God,
holy and mighty,
holy immortal one,
have mercy on us.

The cross that held the Savior of the world.
Holy God,
holy and mighty,
holy immortal one,
have mercy on us.

The cross that held the Savior of the world.
Holy God,
holy and mighty,
holy immortal one,
have mercy on us.

My people, my people,
why have you forsaken me?
Answer me!
I delivered you from captivity
through the water of baptism;
but you handed me over to my captors,
giving me up to die;
and you have made a cross for your Savior.
Lord, have mercy.

I fed you in the wilderness
with the bread of life from heaven;
but you are consumed with desire,
biting and devouring one another;
and you have made a cross for your Savior.
Lord, have mercy.

I claimed you as my family,
as branches of my vine;
but you cut off my chosen ones,
spilling innocent blood;
and you have made a cross for your Savior.
Lord, have mercy.

I spoke to you my Word,
the promise of my love for all;
but you silence my prophets,
refusing to hear my voice;
and you have made a cross for your Savior.
Lord, have mercy.

I came to be your light,
to overcome the darkness;
but you remain in the shadows,
hiding your light from the world;
and you have made a cross for your Savior.
Lord, have mercy.

I gave you the keys to my realm
and welcomed you inside;
but you turn away strangers,
closing the doors that I open;
and you have made a cross for your Savior.
Lord, have mercy.

I offered you my peace
and clothed you with compassion;
but you divide my garments,
tearing apart what I design;
and you have made a cross for your Savior.
Lord, have mercy.

I sent my Holy Spirit
to empower you with grace;
but you trust your own devices,
squandering my good gifts;
and you have made a cross for your Savior.
Lord, have mercy.

I came to dwell among you
as the Word made flesh;
but you ignore neighbors in need,
failing to recognize my face;
and you have made a cross for your Savior.
Lord, have mercy.

Questions for Reflection

Why is this Friday called good? Is the suffering and death of Jesus
something we can and should lament, in the spirit of Psalm 22:1: "My
God, my God, why have you forsaken me?" Is this event something we can
and should celebrate, in the spirit of Psalm 22:31, "[God] has done it" (cf.
John 19:30, "It is finished")? How is it possible both to renounce the evil
of Jesus' crucifixion and to rejoice in the saving mystery of his death and
resurrection?

Household Prayer: Morning

In you, O God,
our ancestors trusted;
they cried to you,
and you delivered them.
Hear my cry this day
and deliver me from evil,
until I rise to meet you
on the day of resurrection. Amen.

Household Prayer: Evening

On you, O God,
I was cast from birth;
since my mother bore me
you have been my God.
Keep me safe this night
and hold me at your breast,
until I rise to meet you
on the day of resurrection. Amen.

Easter Day

Acts 10:34–43
or Isaiah 25:6–9
Psalm 118:1–2, 14–24

1 Corinthians 15:1–11
or Acts 10:34–43
John 20:1–18
or Mark 16:1–8

OPENING WORDS / CALL TO WORSHIP

Alleluia! Christ is risen!
Christ is risen, indeed! Alleluia!
This is the day that the Lord has made;   *Ps. 118:24*
let us rejoice and be glad in it.
Alleluia! Christ is risen!
Christ is risen, indeed! Alleluia!

CALL TO CONFESSION

*[It is especially appropriate on Easter Day to use a Thanksgiving
for Baptism (pp. 192–93) in place of the confessional sequence.]*
Jesus' rising from the dead assures us
that we, too, have been given new life.
Let us repent of our sin before God and one another,
certain of God's mercy.

PRAYER OF CONFESSION

All-knowing, all-powerful God,
we confess that, even on this most holy day,
we are unable to believe in the victory over death
shown to us in the resurrection of Jesus Christ, our Lord.
We confess our utter dependence on you not only for life
but also for faith, hope, and love.
Without your astonishing appearance to our ancestors
and your stunning presence throughout the ages,
we would be lost.
Forgive us and transform us,
that in every way our work and prayer will
make whole what is broken and give peace on earth. Amen.

DECLARATION OF FORGIVENESS

By the grace of God and the witness of our ancestors,
the good news of Jesus' resurrection is our rock and
    our salvation.
You shall not die but live.   *Ps. 118:17*
The rejected cornerstone has become your strength and
    your song.   *Ps. 118:14*
As a called and ordained minister of the church of Christ,
I declare to you the forgiveness of all your sins,
in the name of the Father, Son, and Holy Spirit, one God,
who lives and reigns as Mother of us all, now and forever.

PRAYER OF THE DAY

Holy One, you come to us with power beyond all knowing.
You lift all things out of the dust,
you breathe love into every cell,
you call us into communion with you,
and you claim victory over death.
Blessed be your holy name now and forever. **Amen.**

PRAYER FOR ILLUMINATION

Open our eyes and soften our hearts, O God,
through the work of your Holy Spirit,
that in the hearing of your Word
we may receive new life. **Amen.**

PRAYERS OF INTERCESSION

Let us pray for the church, the world, and all in need, saying,
God in your mercy, hear our prayer.

With joy, we pray for all Christian assemblies
united this morning at the empty tomb.
Help us see you, O God, in those we do not expect to encounter
and remove all fear from our hearts.
God in your mercy, **hear our prayer.**

With gratitude, we give you thanks
for our newly baptized sisters and brothers in every land.
Guide them and keep them,
open their eyes again and again to your blessings.
God in your mercy, **hear our prayer.**

With humility, we pray for this planet, our home.
Heal what we have scarred and broken;
renew the face of Earth from north to south, from east to west
so that your creation may speak to us of your goodness.
God in your mercy, **hear our prayer.**

With hope and love, we pray for the nations of the world,
especially those places overwhelmed by war and conflict
[name here nations in need].
By the light of the resurrection,
destroy the shroud that is cast over all who live under dictatorship,
in the clutches of propagandists, and in ignorance.
Bless peacemakers who work to bring justice
to their country, city, village, and household.
God in your mercy, **hear our prayer.**

With compassion, wipe away the tears of all who weep.
Give us the spiritual tools we need to feed the hungry,
clothe the naked, and comfort those who are in any trouble.
Send your angels to watch over the vulnerable and sick.
God in your mercy, **hear our prayer.**

Hear now the prayers of this assembly spoken aloud or in silence. . . .
[A time of silence is kept.]
God in your mercy, **hear our prayer.**

With fondness, we remember those who saw our risen Lord
and witnessed to his resurrection so that we might have faith.
May their words and deeds inspire us
to sing our "Alleluia!" again and again.
God in your mercy, **hear our prayer.**

Passing from darkness to light,
from bondage to freedom, from death to life,
we commend to you, gracious and ever-living God,
all for whom we pray. **Amen.**

INVITATION TO THE OFFERING

With compassion for our needs,
the Risen One stands beside us, calling our names.

Let us, with that same mercy,
bring forth tithes and offerings to relieve the suffering of this world
and to proclaim far and wide the good news of resurrection life.

PRAYER OF THANKSGIVING/DEDICATION

Holy God, you shower us with gifts so abundant,
we cannot measure them all.
You give us life itself
and the power to befriend our companions in this world.
Bless these gifts for the sake of those in need,
in the name of the Creator, Redeemer, and Sanctifier,
one God, now and forever. **Amen.**

CHARGE

Go from here renewed and strong,
knowing that the Lord is alive, almighty, and present.
Look for the blessings that await you this week.
Weep with those who weep.
Rejoice with those who celebrate.
Tell the story of hope.

BLESSING

Now may the truth of the empty tomb—
the astonishing reality of Jesus' resurrection—
keep you fearless and sure
that you will see the Resurrected One
again and again in this life.
May the power of God's endless love
surround you and guide you,
this day and always.

Questions for Reflection

Paul's claim about Christ Jesus in 1 Corinthians 15 is a creed: Christ died, was buried, was raised, and appeared to many disciples and finally to Paul, who writes, "by the grace of God I am what I am" (v. 10). If you were to say those words of yourself, what would it mean that everything about you—all you are and have done—is "by the grace of God"? Where is God's grace evident in your life today?

Household Prayer: Morning

Heavenly God, our Father,
I am full of thanks for a night of rest
and for this new day and all that now awaits me.
I go forward toward encounters with family and friends,
work and play,
and all that will bring me into contact with strangers,
certain that you are with me.
Lead and guide me in the way of a resurrected life.
Help me to see the risen Lord today; in Jesus' name. Amen.

Household Prayer: Evening

Holy God, our Mother,
you are my comfort at the end as at the beginning of each day.
You pull me toward the goodness you desire for me.
I give you thanks for all that has come my way this day,
and I ask your enveloping power to watch over me this night.
Give rest to all your people.
Wherever there is pain and struggle,
may your holy angels bring peace; in Jesus' name. Amen.

Second Sunday of Easter

Acts 4:32–35   1 John 1:1–2:2
Psalm 133   John 20:19–31

OPENING WORDS / CALL TO WORSHIP

Peace be with you.   *Ps. 133:1–3;*
How good and pleasant it is   *John 20:21–22*
when we live together in unity.
Receive the Holy Spirit.
It is like precious oil on the head,
the blessing of the Lord.

CALL TO CONFESSION

[Water is poured into the font.]
If we say that we have no sin,   *1 John 1:8–9*
we deceive ourselves,
and the truth is not in us.
But if we confess our sins,
God who is faithful and just
will forgive us our sins
and cleanse us from all unrighteousness.

Trusting in God's mercy,
let us confess our sin.

PRAYER OF CONFESSION

You have shown yourself to us, O God,   *John 20:19–31*
by Word and Spirit,
with signs and wonders,
in flesh and blood,
yet we still struggle to live and believe
the good news of Jesus Christ.

151

Have mercy on us; forgive us.
Enter into our lives
and cast out our fear
so that we may come to trust in you
and have life in Jesus' name. Amen.

DECLARATION OF FORGIVENESS
[Water is lifted from the font.]
We have an advocate with God—   *1 John 2:1–2*
Jesus Christ, the righteous one—
who offered his life in love
to save the world from sin.

This is the good news of the gospel:
in Jesus Christ we are forgiven.
Thanks be to God.

PRAYER OF THE DAY
Breathe in this place, O Lord,   *John 20:19, 22*
by the power of your Holy Spirit,
to open our minds,
unlock our hearts,
and enliven our faith
so that we may welcome
the risen one among us. **Amen.**

PRAYER FOR ILLUMINATION
God of all who doubt and believe,   *1 John 1:1; John 20:27–28*
by the gift of your Spirit
enable us to hear with our ears,
to see with our eyes,
and to touch with our hands
your Word of life—Jesus Christ—
our Lord and our God. **Amen.**

PRAYERS OF INTERCESSION
[A time of silence may be kept after each ellipsis.]
Living God, giver of life,   *Ps. 133:2–3;*
hear us as we pray, saying,   *John 20:21–22*
Pour out your blessing, O Lord;
send us your Spirit of peace.

We pray for the church. . . .
Let your church be a living sign
of the woundedness and healing of Christ,
sharing the gift of forgiveness
and the gospel of reconciliation.
Pour out your blessing, O Lord;
send us your Spirit of peace.

We pray for the earth. . . .
Help us to see the scars of death
that mark your good creation,
and to seek the blessing of life
that you offer to all creatures.
Pour out your blessing, O Lord;
send us your Spirit of peace.

We pray for all nations. . . .
Show us how good and pleasant it is
when people live together in unity,
and anoint us with your wisdom
so that we may seek the ways of life.
Pour out your blessing, O Lord;
send us your Spirit of peace.

We pray for this community. . . .
Give us a vision of the common good:
not clinging to our own possessions
but seeking the fullness of life for all
as a testimony to Christ's resurrection.
Pour out your blessing, O Lord;
send us your Spirit of peace.

We pray for loved ones. . . .
Be near to those who walk in darkness
and lead us all into Christ's light
so that our fellowship may be true
and our joy may be complete.
Pour out your blessing, O Lord;
send us your Spirit of peace.

By the blessing of your Spirit,
help us to live as we pray
so that the world may come to know
the gift of life in Christ our Lord. **Amen.**

INVITATION TO THE OFFERING

Remember the first believers—   *Acts 4:32–35*
who shared one heart and soul,
held their possessions in common,
and distributed them to all in need.
In that same spirit,
let us present our offerings
at the feet of the risen Lord.

PRAYER OF THANKSGIVING/DEDICATION

Holy God, we give you thanks and praise   *John 20:19–22*
for light and life and love, and—above all—
the presence of the living Lord among us.
By your Spirit who breathes within us,
strengthen our faith, use our gifts,
and work in our lives to bear witness
to the resurrection of Christ our Lord,
in whose name we pray. **Amen.**

CHARGE

Let your life be a sign of Christ's life   *John 20:29–31*
so that others may come to believe
that the Lord is risen indeed. **Amen.**

BLESSING

This is the blessing of the Lord: *Ps. 133:3*
life forevermore. **Alleluia!**

Questions for Reflection

It all happened on Sunday. It was on "the first day of the week" (John
20:19)—the same day Jesus rose from the dead (John 20:1)—when the
risen Lord appeared to a group of disciples in a locked house and offered
them the gift of the Holy Spirit. Then, one week later (John 20:26), Jesus
came again to the disciples (still shut inside the house), this time allowing

Thomas to see and touch his hands and side. Think about the place where you gather for worship on Sunday. Is it open to the surprising presence of Christ and the liberating gifts of the Spirit? (If not, does the Spirit still move? Does Jesus show up anyway?) Are there times when your questions and doubts grow deeper? Are there times when your faith is strengthened and renewed?

Household Prayer: Morning

God of light, I praise you
for the gift of this new day.
By the power of your Spirit
enable me to live in your light
and seek the holy fellowship
of Jesus Christ my Lord. Amen.

Household Prayer: Evening

Be with me, Lord Jesus,
at the evening of this day.
Enter into my heart
and fill it with your peace
so that I may rejoice and rest
in your presence. Amen.

Third Sunday of Easter

Acts 3:12–19   1 John 3:1–7
Psalm 4   Luke 24:36b–48

OPENING WORDS / CALL TO WORSHIP
The bread of life opens our eyes.
The word of life opens our ears.
The risen one shows us God's own brokenness,
and by those wounds we are healed.
Peace be with you.   *Luke 24:36*
And also with you.

CALL TO CONFESSION
The One who calls us to repent, hears us.
In trust that our Creator knows us through and through,
let us open our hearts to the healing of God's forgiveness.

PRAYER OF CONFESSION
Good and gracious God,
we are creatures of dust,
ignorant of your revelation,
misunderstanding your life, death, and resurrection among us,
needing forgiveness.
We repent of our failure to give as you have given to us.
We beg your mercy for our fallen world.
We seek your Word, that we may live with the faith of Jesus.
Be our solace in this life and always.
We ask this as your own children, holy and incomplete.
Forgive us and lead us. Amen.

DECLARATION OF FORGIVENESS

In the name of God, the Father, Son, and Holy Spirit,
your plea for absolution has been heard.
God's promises are sure: your sins are forgiven.
Peace be with you.

PRAYER OF THE DAY

Almighty God, your power makes the lame walk
and the dead rise to new life.
We give you thanks for the love poured into our world
through Christ Jesus,
who opened our minds to understand what you have made,
whose appearance among his followers brings peace,
and who creates faith through touch and taste.
Show us Jesus, even now,
through the mystery of your threefold presence,
one God, abiding now and forever. **Amen.**

PRAYER FOR ILLUMINATION

Holy God, by your Spirit
reveal your radical, surprising love;
come to us through your holy word,
and let us hear what you are saying. **Amen.**

PRAYERS OF INTERCESSION

God has made the One who was rejected
the cornerstone of a new community.
In the name of Christ Jesus,
let us pray for the needs of the world, saying,
Hear us, O God, your mercy is great.

Holy One,
as the risen Christ opened the minds of the disciples
    to understand the Scriptures
and gave them power through the Holy Spirit
    to walk boldly in this world,
open your people today to the healing, wisdom, and faith
    given in your Word;
hear us, O God, **your mercy is great.**

Prince of Peace,
as Christ Jesus showed his wounded hands and feet
to the terrified apostles,
reveal to your church, and to people of prayer in every faith,
the wounds of our neighbors, the fears of individuals and families,
and the avenues toward healing;
hear us, O God, **your mercy is great.**

Author of life,
we beg for peace among nations,
peace throughout communities,
peace within families.
Guide leaders and voters,
legislatures and parliaments,
judges and juries.
Teach diplomacy and let our ways be formed
so that all creatures, plants, and people may have plenty;
hear us, O God, **your mercy is great.**

Light in our darkness,
let your brightness burn in places shrouded in violence.
Reveal the pains that are hidden in secret.
Unveil the needs of our own hearts
so that we may know the power of vulnerability.
Your Son was raised to life even from the grave.
Show us again that life comes from death;
hear us, O God, **your mercy is great.**

Healer of our every ill,
we pray for all who are in need,
for refugees of war and all who are displaced by storms,
for rescue workers and medical teams,
for those whose bones are weary,
for those who show us the power of community
to give hope to the frightened,
and for all who have asked for our prayers;
hear us, O God, **your mercy is great.**

You command us to bring to you our deepest desires, O God,
and we pray now for those persons and concerns

that lie on our hearts, spoken aloud or in silence. . . .
[A time of silence is kept.]
Hear us, O God, **your mercy is great.**

Trusting in your abundant mercy, O God,
we commend into your care all for whom we pray,
and our own lives;
through Jesus Christ, our Savior. **Amen.**

INVITATION TO THE OFFERING

As Jesus gave himself fully for us
and then appeared to the disciples bringing peace,
so let us now bring wholeness and healing to others
through our tithes and gifts.

PRAYER OF THANKSGIVING/DEDICATION

Lord God, we offer to you only a portion
of what you have given us.
All that we have is from your creative hand.
All that we can give away we do through Jesus' love.
All our renewal comes from the Holy Spirit's wisdom.
Deal graciously with these gifts so that others may have joy;
in Jesus' name. **Amen.**

CHARGE

The word of God assures us:
What we will be has not yet been revealed.   *1 John 3:2*
Live, therefore, with hope,
share your joy,
withhold your anger,
shed your disappointments,
turn to all people with gentleness.

BLESSING

The Lord bless and keep you,
shine upon you with grace and mercy,
and give you what is needed for each new day.

Questions for Reflection

When Jesus appeared to the disciples, "he opened their minds to understand the scriptures" (Luke 24:45). What is it to "understand" God's word? How does understanding feed your faith? In the coming week, take note of one new understanding that comes to you from something you hear or read or realize through another person.

Household Prayer: Morning

God of surprising revelations, I thank you for rest and renewal.
I thank you that when you come to your people,
you speak peace and invite faith in you.
Make this new day a time when I will give more thanks for life
    than I did yesterday.
Give me ears to hear your will for me,
hands that are open to others,
and eyes to see the beauty in your world; in Jesus' name. Amen.

Household Prayer: Evening

For all that has happened this day, O God, I give you thanks.
Even for the obstacles I faced, I thank you.
Especially when I wobbled in doubt, I thank you because I did not fall.
You came to hold me strong and help me take the next step.
Now give me rest, secure in your never-failing arms.
Let my dreams revolve around what is pleasing and good,
bringing me to a new day with zeal for your gifts; in Jesus' name. Amen.

Fourth Sunday of Easter

Acts 4:5–12   1 John 3:16–24
Psalm 23   John 10:11–18

OPENING WORDS / CALL TO WORSHIP

The Lord Jesus Christ is our shepherd.   *Ps. 23:1; John 10:14–16*
He lays down his life for his sheep.
The Lord Jesus Christ is our shepherd.
He knows us, and we belong to him.
The Lord Jesus Christ is our shepherd.
He speaks, and we listen for his voice.

CALL TO CONFESSION

[Pouring water into the font]
If we are honest with ourselves,   *1 John 3:20*
our hearts condemn us.
But God, who knows everything,
is greater than our hearts;
and God's deep desire for us
is mercy, love, and peace.
Therefore let us confess our sin.

PRAYER OF CONFESSION

Lord, have mercy on us.   *1 John 3:16–24*
We talk about love,
but our actions betray us.
We talk about love,
but we neglect the poor.
We talk about love,
but we fail to love one another.
Lord, have mercy on us.

Forgive us, and abide in us
by the power of your Spirit
so that our lives may show
our love for Jesus Christ,
in whose body we live
and in whose name we pray. Amen.

DECLARATION OF FORGIVENESS

[Lifting water from the font]
We seek God's grace with boldness   *1 John 3:16, 21–22*
because we trust in Jesus Christ,
the One who loves us
and laid down his life for us.
This is the good news of the gospel:
in Jesus Christ we are forgiven.
Thanks be to God.

PRAYER OF THE DAY

[At the font, pulpit, or table]
We are your people, O God—   *Ps. 23*
the sheep of your pasture,
the flock you have gathered.
Lead us beside still waters;
teach us the way of righteousness;
and feed us at your table;
through Jesus Christ,
our good shepherd. **Amen.**

PRAYER FOR ILLUMINATION

Lord God, good shepherd,   *Ps. 23:3, 6; John 10:16*
by the leading of your Spirit,
help us to listen for your voice
and follow in your paths
all the days of our lives;
in Jesus' name. **Amen.**

PRAYERS OF INTERCESSION

[A time of silence may follow each ellipsis.]
With boldness, let us offer our prayers   *Ps. 23:6; 1 John 3:21–24*
to the shepherd of our souls, saying,
God of goodness and mercy, hear our prayer.

We pray for the church in every place. . . .
Gather us together and make us one,
one in ministry and mission to the world,
so that there will be one flock, one shepherd.
God of goodness and mercy, **hear our prayer.**

We pray for the nations of the world. . . .
Anoint all leaders with your wisdom
so that they will use their power
to help the poor and defend the vulnerable.
God of goodness and mercy, **hear our prayer.**

We pray for this community. . . .
Strengthen those who work each day
to heal the sick, welcome the outcasts,
and help sisters and brothers in need.
God of goodness and mercy, **hear our prayer.**

We pray for friends and loved ones. . . .
Comfort all who are suffering;
walk with them through dark valleys
and restore them, body, mind, and soul.
God of goodness and mercy, **hear our prayer.**

Loving God, by the power of your Spirit,
help us to keep your commandments
and to love one another with the love of Jesus,
in whose holy name we pray. **Amen.**

INVITATION TO THE OFFERING

How does God's love abide in anyone   *1 John 3:17*
who has the goods of the world
and sees a brother or sister in need,
yet refuses to help?
With love for God and neighbor,
let us offer our lives to the Lord.

PRAYER OF THANKSGIVING/DEDICATION

Gracious God, we give you thanks   *1 John 3:16*
that you have shown us the meaning of love
through Jesus Christ, who gave his life for us.

Show us how to share Christ's love
by giving our lives for one another;
to the glory of your holy name. **Amen.**

CHARGE

In the name of the good shepherd,   *1 John 3:23; John 10:11*
love one another. **Amen.**

BLESSING

May the goodness and mercy of God   *Ps. 23:6*
follow you all the days of your life,
and, at your life's end, may you dwell
in the house of the Lord forever. **Alleluia!**

Questions for Reflection

What does it mean to lay down our lives for one another (1 John 3:16)?
Think about people who have been "good shepherds" for you, sharing the
love and showing the way of Jesus Christ. Who has helped to lead you in
right paths or walked with you in dark valleys? Who has given you comfort
and calmed your fears? Who has shown you hospitality and grace, making
a place at the table for you, even when you felt surrounded by enemies?
How have you done these things for others?

Household Prayer: Morning

Good shepherd, walk beside me
through the joy and trouble of this day,
and lead me in right paths
for your name's sake. Amen.

Household Prayer: Evening

Good shepherd, remain with me
in the dark and stillness of this night,
and let me lie down in safety
to restore my soul. Amen.

Fifth Sunday of Easter

Acts 8:26–40   1 John 4:7–21
Psalm 22:25–31   John 15:1–8

OPENING WORDS / CALL TO WORSHIP
In the wilderness, water brings life.
Seek us out, O God, and take us to the water.
In the Word of God, the good news gives light.
Seek us out, O God, and fill us with understanding.
In the bread and the wine, the body of our Savior
    nourishes everyone.
Seek us out, O God, and give us yourself.
Here is the water of life, the word that feeds, the food of eternity.
Come and praise the vine that gives all goodness.

CALL TO CONFESSION
Trusting in the mercy of God,
let us confess to God and to one another
our failure to love our neighbor.

PRAYER OF CONFESSION
God of mercy,
we confess that we have not borne the fruit
    of the Spirit.   *John 15:5*
We have not loved others as you have loved us.
We have denied the promises of baptism
and cut ourselves off from you.
Forgive us, restore us,
that we may abide in your love
and live out your mercy,
for the sake of Jesus Christ,
in whose name we pray. Amen.

165

DECLARATION OF FORGIVENESS

You have already been cleansed by the word that
    God has spoken to you. *John 15:3*
In baptism God claimed you
and joined you to Christ, as branches to a vine.
Believe the promise given to you:
in Jesus Christ, you are forgiven.

PRAYER OF THE DAY

Wondrous Vinegrower, you make all things new
    in water and Word,
feeding your people with love, joy, and peace.
Lead us today and every day to the font of new beginnings.
Teach us to love what you have commanded
and to prune what does not nourish your creation,
in the name of the Creator, Redeemer, and Sustainer,
one God, now and forever. **Amen.**

PRAYER FOR ILLUMINATION

Come, Holy Spirit,
that through your word we may be guided
into the love of God for all the world. **Amen.**

PRAYERS OF INTERCESSION

Let us join with all creation in praying for
    the good of the earth, saying,
God, who makes us one, hear our prayer.

O God, we give you thanks for your Holy Spirit
whose work at creation continues in us.
Through Christ Jesus you have shown your love
    for this earth you made.
We pray that all the world may know your
    power and goodness;
God, who makes us one, **hear our prayer.**

Word of life, reveal the wonder of your world
    to all people.
Show us anew what lives around us, over us,
    beneath us, within us.

Enliven the church with your Spirit,
that we may honor your earth with responsible care.
God, who makes us one, **hear our prayer.**

Almighty God, uphold our sisters and brothers
who endure disasters
caused by weather, war, famine, sickness, or greed.
Strengthen all who are in peril,
especially the people of *[name places of concern].*
You are our refuge and strength, a very present help
    in time of trouble.
God, who makes us one, **hear our prayer.**

Giver of all good things, bring trust and sympathy
to the nations of the world.
Let peacemakers reign wherever there is conflict.
Give wisdom to leaders and hope to the poor.
God, who makes us one, **hear our prayer.**

Good healer, we pray for all who are in need of comfort.
Comfort those who mourn;
uphold those who are sick, or holding vigil,
or awaiting words of hope,
especially those we name now silently or aloud *[silence].*
God, who makes us one, **hear our prayer.**

Trusting in your mercy, we commend to you all those
    we have named
and those whose needs are known only to you,
in the name of your Son, Christ our Lord,
who lives and reigns with you and the Holy Spirit,
one God, now and forever. **Amen.**

INVITATION TO THE OFFERING
Offering what we have for the sake of others
is a discipline of pruning—letting go of our possessions,
our time, and even ourselves—
to extend the gospel witness into the world.
Be generous in your ministry of giving.
You need not fear; you abide in the vine.

PRAYER OF THANKSGIVING/DEDICATION

Through our offerings, O God,
give your loving Spirit to a world in need of comfort.
Make our many gifts one offering for the world;
in the name of Jesus. **Amen.**

CHARGE

Go out with joy that you have been fed and healed,
securely abiding as branches of the true vine.
Go and tell the story of faith
that is given to you by the One who never lets you go.
Seek out those who abound with sacred questions,
and be ready to answer a mystery with love.

BLESSING

As Jesus entered into human life,
his life is still alive in you.
The blessing of Almighty God be upon you
today and always.

Question for Reflection

What is your deepest desire? Jesus says that "whatever you wish . . . it will
be done for you" (John 15:7). Spend time in the next days asking yourself
at evermore profound levels what you most devoutly wish for in this life
and the next. Then ask for it.

Household Prayer: Morning

God of all beginnings, you bring a new day,
and you promise to journey with me through the hours.
I thank you for the breath and strength I have,
and I beg your help that I may use my powers wisely
and with compassion toward everyone I meet.
Let my questions today be a form of pruning
to bring forth in me new understandings,
healing, and good fruit; in Jesus' name. Amen.

Household Prayer: Evening

Sweet Jesus, in this night of rest,
heal my broken places and restore my faith.
You are my vine; only in you am I strong enough
to face the darkness of this world.
I thank you for the safety of my home
and pray for those who have no bed tonight.
Make me grateful,
in the name of the Father, Son, and Holy Spirit,
one God, Mother of us all. Amen.

Sixth Sunday of Easter

Acts 10:44–48   1 John 5:1–6

Psalm 98   John 15:9–17

OPENING WORDS / CALL TO WORSHIP

Sing to our God a new song.   *Ps. 98:1–8*

God has done marvelous things!

Make a joyful noise to the Lord!

Break forth into joyous song and sing praises.

Let the sea roar and all that fills it.

Let the world and its people sing together for joy!

CALL TO CONFESSION

We have been called to follow Christ

by obeying his one commandment:

that we love one another as he has loved us. *John 15:12*

Let us confess how we have fallen short of that love.

PRAYER OF CONFESSION

Loving God, we have not loved you

or each other with our whole hearts.

Forgive us, we pray,

and lead us toward wholeness,

that we may be filled with your joy. *John 15:11*

In Jesus' name we pray. Amen.

DECLARATION OF FORGIVENESS

Christ loves us so much that he

laid down his life for us   *John 15:13*

and calls us his friends.

If we can forgive our friends,

how much more does Christ forgive us!

PRAYER OF THE DAY

Loving God, help us to love others
as Christ has loved us.
Bring us into the spiritual joy
of living our lives as your friend,
and teach us to abide in your love,
that we may show that love to the world. **Amen.**

PRAYER FOR ILLUMINATION

Pour out your Holy Spirit upon us, O God,   *Acts 10:45*
in the reading of your Word,
that we would hear what you have to say to us today.
May your Holy Spirit be poured out upon us;
through Jesus Christ. **Amen.**

PRAYERS OF INTERCESSION

We sing for joy, O God,
for you are coming to judge the world   *Ps. 98:9*
with righteousness and fairness
between nations and between people.

We pray for the poor and the desperate
as well as for those who abuse and oppress them,
both here and abroad.
Comfort those who suffer
and chasten those who cause their suffering,
that your justice may be known in all the earth.

We pray for families, communities, and nations
torn apart by violence.
Heal the broken places
and imbue your earth with peace.

We pray for the sick and the dying,
for those who are friendless and lonely,
for those living with grief or depression.
Bring them your friendship and renew their joy.

We pray for ourselves, your church,
that we may bear fruit of peace, hope, and love,
fruit that will last.   *John 15:16*

Now in the name of your Son, Jesus Christ,
our friend,   *John 15:15*
and in the Holy Spirit poured out on us,   *Acts 10:45*
we sing a new song to praise you
for you are doing marvelous things! **Amen.**   *Ps. 98:1*

INVITATION TO THE OFFERING
Let us show our friendship with Christ
and our love for our neighbors
by giving generously so that
we may bear the lasting fruit of Christ's love.

PRAYER OF THANKSGIVING/DEDICATION
Holy God, in Christ you have chosen us
    to be your friends   *John 15:15*
and to know your will in the world.
Therefore we pray in Jesus' name   *John 15:16*
that these tithes and offerings
spread your love near and far. **Amen.**

CHARGE
Live in the joy of Christ's love   *John 15:11*
and in all the marvelous things that God is doing!   *Ps. 98:1*

BLESSING
May the righteous fairness of God,
the loving friendship of Christ,
and the gift of the Holy Spirit
go with you all.

Question for Reflection

In our Gospel lesson this week, Jesus speaks of his extreme love for us, calls
us his friends, and says that he makes known to us everything that he hears
from God. How does thinking of Christ as our friend and lover—or Lord
and Master—affect our daily living?

Household Prayer: Morning

Holy One, I begin today breathing in your love for me,
for others, and for the world.
Keep me mindful of all the marvelous things
you are doing around and within me today.
Help me to feel my friendship with Jesus
and his confidence in me.
Maintain in my heart the image of myself as a tree,
bearing the fruit of Christ's love everywhere I go today. Amen.

Household Prayer: Evening

God, you are both judge and friend.
Even as I review my day,
I give it over to you.
I let go of the good, the bad, and the in-between,
trusting in your care for me.
I am content this night to abide in your love.
I breathe in your joy and your peace.
Whatever I need, I ask of you in Jesus' name. Amen.

Ascension of the Lord

Acts 1:1–11   Ephesians 1:15–23
Psalm 47 *or* Psalm 93   Luke 24:44–53

OPENING WORDS / CALL TO WORSHIP
I have heard of your faith in the Lord Jesus   *Eph. 1:15–20*
and your love toward one another.
So I do not cease to give thanks for you
as I remember you in my prayers.
I pray that the God of our Lord Jesus Christ
may give you a spirit of wisdom and revelation
as you come to know him.
With the eyes of our hearts enlightened,
we see the greatness of Christ's power
at work in us who believe.
God put this power to work in Christ
when God raised him from the dead—
and seated him at God's right hand
in the glory of the heavenly places!

CALL TO CONFESSION
God-lovers, let us repent of those things
that have drawn us away from God and our neighbors,
that we may receive the joy of forgiveness.

PRAYER OF CONFESSION
God, lover of humankind,
you have asked us to
proclaim your name to all people.   *Luke 24:47*
We confess that we have held back
from doing that, shy and self-conscious.
Forgive us, we pray, and
empower us in Jesus' name. Amen.

174

DECLARATION OF FORGIVENESS

The promise of our faith is that
we are already forgiven and,
in Christ's name, given the power
to rise up and subdue
all that separates us from God and each other.
Receive the Holy Spirit and be
empowered to be witnesses
of God's resurrection power
in Jesus Christ.

PRAYER OF THE DAY

We thank you, almighty God,
for the life of Jesus among us,
and that he reigns in power for us.
Strengthen our hope
and bless the work of our hands,
that we may live as his body in this world.
In Jesus' name we ask it. **Amen.**

PRAYER FOR ILLUMINATION

Enlighten the eyes of our hearts, O God,   *Eph. 1:17–18*
and grant us a spirit of wisdom and revelation
through the reading of this, your Word. **Amen.**

PRAYERS OF INTERCESSION

Let us pray for the whole world and everything in it,
for there is much need and want,
and we, the church, have been called to be
Christ's body in our world today.
May we be Christ's body,
the fullness of him who fills all in all.   *Eph. 1:23*

We pray for all the people of the world,
especially those who live in want and need.
May we be Christ's body,
the fullness of him who fills all in all.

We pray for the nations of the world,
especially their leaders,

that they may see, understand, and honor
the sovereignty of peace and compassion
over their own self-interest.
May we be Christ's body,
the fullness of him who fills all in all.

We pray for the ill and the abused,
and for all those who need protection and care.
May we be Christ's body,
the fullness of him who fills all in all.

We pray for the earth and its delicate
yet life-giving ecosystem.
By the same power through which you
resurrected Christ,
empower us to restore endangered species,
polluted waters, and unclean air.
May we be Christ's body,
the fullness of him who fills all in all.

We pray for your church and
its called and elected leaders.
May we all grow in faith and love,   *Eph. 1:1*
and know with surety
the inheritance and hope to which you have called us.   *Eph. 1:18*
May we be Christ's body,
the fullness of him who fills all in all.

Holy, holy, holy God,
your power and majesty fill the universe,
far above all we see and do, measure and name.   *Eph. 1:21*
You reign with Christ and the Holy Spirit,
one God, forever and ever. **Amen.**

INVITATION TO THE OFFERING
Christ has called us to be   *Acts 1:8*
his witnesses to the ends of the earth.
So let us give generously to fulfill that call.

PRAYER OF THANKSGIVING/DEDICATION

Holy One, we clap our hands and shout for joy!   *Ps. 47:1*
We give you praise and these offerings,
for, with Christ ascended by your side,   *Eph. 1:20*
you are God, awesome and Most High! **Amen.**   *Ps. 47:2*

CHARGE

Grow together in faith and love,   *Eph. 1:15*
being the church,
which is Christ's body,
the fullness of him who fills all in all.   *Eph. 1:23*

BLESSING

Go forth knowing   *Eph. 1:18–19*
the hope to which God has called you,
the glorious inheritance that you have received,
and God's power that is at work for us
through Jesus Christ in the unity of the Holy Spirit.

Questions for Reflection

The Ascension of Christ to be seated at the right hand of God is a grand liturgical celebration in the life of the church. It marks forty days of celebrating Easter and God's triumph over the powers of oppression, depression, and our fear of death through the resurrection of Jesus Christ. It is one of many images we have for Christ: good shepherd, suffering servant, great physician. How does the image of the ascended Christ affect your understanding of who he is? What are the strengths and weaknesses in this image of Christ for you?

Household Prayer: Morning

Holy One, come into my heart this morning
and give me eyes to see throughout this day
all the ways that you rule.
Put your resurrecting power to work in my life
and empower me to be a witness to Christ,
that my life may be a song of thanksgiving to you. Amen.

God, embrace me now at the end of this day.
As in every day, there have been ups and downs,
joys and disappointments.
I thank you for my faith that, above it all, you rule.
I put my trust in you as I give this day, now spent, to you.
Do with it what you will, and send your Holy Spirit
to pull forward threads from today
that you will spin into good things tomorrow.
I pray through Jesus Christ, who reigns with you,
now and forever. Amen.

Seventh Sunday of Easter

Acts 1:15–17, 21–26   1 John 5:9–13
Psalm 1   John 17:6–19

OPENING WORDS / CALL TO WORSHIP

Happy are those who do not ridicule and scoff   *Ps. 1:1–3*
but who delight in God's teachings
and meditate on them day and night.
They are like trees planted by streams of water.
They yield fruit in due season,
and their leaves do not wither.

CALL TO CONFESSION

The Lord watches over our ways.   *Ps. 1:6*
Let us put our trust in God's grace
and confess our sins.

PRAYER OF CONFESSION

God, though you call us to delight in
your teachings,
we can become cynical and full of doubt.
Do not judge us, we pray, but heal us
and restore us to you.
Guard us and protect us from evil,   *John 17:15, 17*
and sanctify us in truth;
in Jesus' name. Amen.

DECLARATION OF FORGIVENESS

In Christ Jesus, God has promised
to forgive us and reconcile us to God and each other.
With joy, let us share that peace with one another.

PRAYER OF THE DAY

Holy One,
open us to the possibility that we are being chosen
to be new disciples with new ministries
in Jesus' name. **Amen.**

PRAYER FOR ILLUMINATION

May the reading of your Word
sanctify us in the truth and   *John 17:17*
bring us to perfect joy. **Amen.**   *John 17:13*

PRAYERS OF INTERCESSION

Let us pray for the world
and ask that we may be given the grace
to be faithful disciples of Jesus.   *Acts 1:25*
May we be like trees planted by streams of water.   *Ps. 1:3*

Holy God, this world is peopled by
those who delight in your teachings
and those who scoff at your ways.   *Ps. 1:1–2*
Guide us to meditate on you day and night,   *Ps. 1:2*
that we may be an influence for good in the world.
May we be like trees planted by streams of water.

We pray for the people and the leaders of the world
in all our diversity.
Sanctify them in your truth,
that there may be peace and harmony on earth.
May we be like trees planted by streams of water.

We pray for those who are sick or suffering,
that they may know your protection and care
through our faithful service.
May we be like trees planted by streams of water.

We pray for your church,
that by the marriage of your grace and our faith
we may serve you and our neighbors.
May we be like trees planted by streams of water.

We pray for Earth itself, your marvelous creation.
Inspire and help us to be the good stewards
that you ask us to be, now and for the future.
May we be like trees planted by streams of water.

Make holy all for which we pray—
the poor, the infirm, the church, the world—
for holiness and wholeness come from you.
Receive these prayers both spoken and unspoken,
for we are yours. **Amen.**

INVITATION TO THE OFFERING
God invites us to give the
testimony of our hearts   *1 John 5:10*
in practical offerings of money and time.
Therefore let us testify to God's love
by bringing our gifts.

PRAYER OF THANKSGIVING/DEDICATION
Jesus has made God known to us.   *John 17:6*
We already belong to God.
And so we dedicate these gifts to God's service
and to the glory of God's name. **Amen.**

CHARGE
Living in the love of Christ,
be open to God calling you
into a new ministry.

BLESSING
Jesus Christ has already given us
into the arms of a loving God.
Therefore go in the Spirit of peace.

Questions for Reflection

In the first chapter of Acts, when the eleven seek to replace Judas with a
new apostle, they ask God to reveal who that should be by casting lots.
How do you think God's will is revealed to us today? Is it revealed in more
than one way?

Household Prayer: Morning

Holy One, thank you for the ability to begin my day in prayer.
Guide my path today.
No matter what happens, help me to feel that I belong to you,
and bring me home to you at the end of the day. Amen.

Household Prayer: Evening

Loving God, thank you for claiming me as your own.
I have been in the world all day,
but I also know that I am in you.
Give me the grace to let go of this day
and entrust it to your care.
Be with me as I sleep this night
and continue to sanctify me in your embrace. Amen.

Day of Pentecost

Acts 2:1–21
or Ezekiel 37:1–14
Psalm 104:24–34, 35b

Romans 8:22–27
or Acts 2:1–21
John 15:26–27;
16:4b–15

OPENING WORDS / CALL TO WORSHIP

God declares: "I will pour out my Spirit upon all flesh.   *Acts 2:17, 21*
Your sons and your daughters shall prophesy.
The young shall see visions.
The elders shall dream dreams.
Both men and women shall prophesy.
And everyone who calls on the name of the Lord
    shall be saved."

CALL TO CONFESSION

Let us call on the name of the One who invites us
to speak the truth about ourselves and our relationships
and promises to show us mercy.

PRAYER OF CONFESSION

Holy and Merciful God,
we do not know how to pray as we ought,   *Rom. 8:26*
and we know too well our constant failures
to do as you have commanded
and to hold fast to your word.
Forgive us for the divisions we nurture,
guide us to your way,
keep us in your care, and
lead us into faith.
We trust your word that the Spirit of truth
will show us all things
and grant us courage and peace. Amen.

DECLARATION OF FORGIVENESS

People of God, body of Christ, sisters and brothers,
the Spirit of God's truth has come upon creation and upon you,
to interpret the mysteries of eternal time.
Through the power of the Holy Spirit,
in the name of Christ Jesus, our Savior,
and by the authority of the church,
I declare to you the complete forgiveness of your sin.
Be at peace with one another because of God's mercy.

PRAYER OF THE DAY

Gracious God, you come among your people
as One who fashioned all things,
who, face-to-face, revealed your knowledge of our lives,
and whose presence brings assurance and hope.
Pour out upon us the Spirit of your love
so that in hearing and seeing the gifts of this life,
we may know the way to live in thanksgiving;
through Jesus Christ, our Lord. **Amen.**

PRAYER FOR ILLUMINATION

Holy Spirit, come again.
As long ago you inspired, astonished, and confused the people,
come to us now to
fill our ears with the sound of your breath,
fill our eyes with the brilliance of your presence in each other,
fill our hearts with your good Word. **Amen.**

PRAYERS OF INTERCESSION

Let us pray for the church, the world, and all in need, saying,
hear us, O God, your mercy is great.

In gratitude for all that you have done for us, Holy God, we pray:
For the people of God in every land;
for those who continually teach the faith;
for witnesses who by their example show your steadfast love;
for all who are estranged from the church;
and for the strength to walk in your ways
and observe your command;
hear us, O God, **your mercy is great.**

For nations, communities, and families torn by violence;
for leaders and protesters, for managers and visionaries;
for dictators and peacemakers;
for the allies of our nation and for our enemies;
especially today for the people of *[insert contemporary concerns]*;
hear us, O God, **your mercy is great.**

For Earth and its riches;
for soil and wetlands, trees, bushes, rivers and lakes, oceans and air;
and for all the peoples who inhabit this great creation;
for the ability to choose life for all creatures
and to honor the welfare of generations to come;
hear us, O God, **your mercy is great.**

For all people who are victims of injustice;
for those who are unemployed or underemployed;
for those living on the streets of our cities;
for everyone affected by divorce;
for people struggling with addiction, anger, fear, or illness;
for all who have asked this congregation for prayer;
for those we name now aloud or in our hearts *[silence]*;
hear us, O God, **your mercy is great.**

For this community of faith;
for those who come to worship every week
and those who cannot come;
for the young and the old;
for newcomers and long-familiar faces;
for the newly baptized in every land;
for those who are seeking to know you;
hear us, O God, **your mercy is great.**

For all else that this assembly is concerned with today,
named aloud or in our hearts *[silence]*;
hear us, O God, **your mercy is great.**

Thanksgiving for all the saints who served you in life
and whose proclamation of the gospel continues to renew the church;
hear us, O God, **your mercy is great.**

Into your promises, we entrust all those
whose needs are known to us today
and those whose needs are only known to you.
Grant peace to all, through your Son, Jesus Christ, our Lord,
in the unity of the Holy Spirit, one God, now and forever. **Amen.**

INVITATION TO THE OFFERING

The Holy Spirit was sent to increase our compassion
and to make us glad to spread good news by caring for those in need.
May you enter into the discipline of giving
as a work of the Holy Spirit within you.

PRAYER OF THANKSGIVING/DEDICATION

God of mercy, we give you thanks for all that your bounty creates.
The gifts we bring today acknowledge our debt to you
and our intent to relieve others of their burdens.
Bless what we offer and bless those who will be shown
deeds of power through them;
in Jesus' name. **Amen.**

CHARGE

Jesus did not leave us without hope
but sent the Holy Spirit to nurture faith and love in this world.
Live this vision in all that you do:
respond to rancor with kindness,
be patient where there is pain,
and let your dreams become reality.
Peace be with you.

BLESSING

The Holy Spirit has come to inhabit this world
with freedom, truth, and understanding.
You are not alone.
May God keep you and make your prayers bear fruit.

Questions for Reflection

In this coming week consider how many ways and through which persons
you are shown a new path for your life. Watch for startling nudges or
sudden epiphanies; listen for sighs that signal letting go of something

pressing so that you can hear the Spirit's guidance. What have you learned? How can you give thanks?

Household Prayer: Morning

God of newness and delight,
you greet your world again with light and life.
I awaken to your presence behind, before, beneath, above, and within me.
I thank you for another day
and ask only that you keep me so firmly in your care
that I can move gracefully through all I have to do.
Guard my family, my friends, and all my brothers and sisters in faith.
Let me be a peacemaker today; in Jesus' name. Amen.

Household Prayer: Evening

Good and Holy One,
you have led me through this day of many encounters
to the time when I may close my eyes and dream.
I thank you for the people you have sent my way today,
for the work I have had to do,
for the food, shelter, and safety you have given.
I pray that people everywhere
may have all necessary comfort and nourishment
and that I may lie down in peace,
resting in the trust that you are watching over all creation.
I pray this in the name of the One who made Earth,
called the children to come,
and blows through our days with wisdom. Amen.

❧ ADDITIONAL RESOURCES ❦

Greetings

Grace and peace in Christ Jesus, our teacher and redeemer.

Blessings to you, servants of God.   *Ps. 134*
We lift up our hands and bless the Lord!

This is the day that our God has made.   *Ps. 118:24*
Let us rejoice and be glad in it!

Give thanks to our God, for God is good!   *Ps. 118:1*
God's steadfast love endures forever!

I greet you in the name of Christ Jesus,   *Eph. 2:14*
who breaks down the dividing walls between us.

Christ has created in himself one new humanity,   *Eph. 2:15, 18, 19*
thus making peace.
Through him we have full access in one Spirit to God.
We are no longer strangers and aliens,
but members of the household of God.

Since we are justified by faith, we have peace with God   *Rom. 5:1–2*
and stand in grace through Jesus Christ.
May the peace of the Lord be always with you.
And also with you.

Jesus said that where two or three of us   *Matt. 18:20*
are gathered in his name, he is among us.
We meet in his name and share in his peace.

Thanksgiving for Baptism

Holy God,
We give you thanks for your grace revealed through water.
Before time, at the beginning of creation,
your Holy Spirit moved across the face of the deep, dark waters
and from chaos you brought forth light and land and every living thing,
declaring them good.

When the world fell into wickedness and rebellion,
you saved Noah in the terrible, scouring flood;
by light refracted in the water of clouds,
you made the rainbow a sign of your covenant
never to abandon the earth and its inhabitants to the destructive curse
    of evil.

You led the Hebrews through the waters of the Red Sea,
freeing them from slavery in Egypt,
and led them through the waters of the Jordan River,
bringing them to your promised land of milk and honey.

To the waters of that same Jordan River,
your Son Jesus came to be baptized by John,
as the Holy Spirit anointed him to proclaim salvation for the world.

Send your Holy Spirit to bless the water of this font.
Let it be for us the water of new creation, the cleansing flood,
the covenant rainbow, the Red Sea of victory, the anointing of salvation.

Let it be our Jordan River,
through which we become one with Jesus Christ in his baptism,
receiving the promise you have opened to people of every time and nation;
for we pray through Christ who lives with you and the Holy Spirit,
one God forever and ever. **Amen.**

Great Prayers of Thanksgiving / Eucharistic Prayers

[These prayers are offered as supplementary resources that are intended to be in line with approved and published denominational worship materials. They may be adapted for your congregational context.]

GENERAL USE

God be with you.
And also with you.
Let us open our hearts.
We open them to our God.
Let us give thanks to the Holy One, our God.
It is right to give our thanks and praise.

It is a right and good and joyful thing,
always and everywhere,
to give you thanks, All-Loving God,
creator of energy and matter,
heaven and earth.

When there was nothing,
you created all that is.
In due time you made for humans to evolve
and gave us the power of language.
When we felt the sting of the lash,
you liberated us.
When we were lost and our souls were faint,
you led us home through prophets and apostles.

When the time was right, you sent your Son
to embody your promise to save us.

Therefore we praise you,
joining the everlasting chorus of
the wind and the streams,
the animals and flowers,
the living and the dead,
the stars and the planets,
and all the company of heaven:

Holy, holy, holy, God of sovereignty and light,
heaven and earth are full of your glory.
Hosanna in the highest.
Blessed is the One who comes in the name of our God.
Hosanna in the highest.

We are grateful for Jesus the Christ,
who teaches and heals us
and becomes the way for us,
through his dying and his rising,
that we may die through him
and rise through him
into a new heaven and a new earth.

We are grateful that on the night before he died,
he took bread and, after giving thanks for it,
broke it and shared it with his companions,
saying, Take, eat,
this is my body, broken for you.
We are grateful that, after the meal was ended,
he took the cup and passed it to them,
as it is now being passed on to us,
and said, Take this cup and drink from it,
all of you—
for this is the cup of the new covenant,
my life poured out for you.
Now when you eat and drink of this,
remember me.

We remember Jesus as we share this meal,
one in the Spirit.

God, bless these simple gifts of the earth—
this bread and this cup—
that they may become for us,
through the power of your Holy Spirit,
Christ's presence with us,
transforming us into
the body of Christ in the world.

May this meal inspire and strengthen us
to love you, each other, and this world
until Christ comes again
and brings all things to their fulfillment.

All glory and honor are yours, Holy One,
through Christ, in the Spirit,
now and always. **Amen.**

ADVENT

God be with you.
And also with you.
Let us open our hearts.
We open them to our God.
Let us give thanks to the Holy One, our God.
It is right to lift up thanks and praise.

Great Deliverer, how wondrous are your deeds!   *Acts 2:11*
You created the world
and all that is in it.
With a mighty arm you parted the waters   *Exod. 14:21*
and led your people to liberation.
When we were in exile,
you gathered us up in your bosom   *Isa. 40:11*
and led us home like a mother sheep.
When we were mistreating our own,   *Luke 3:10*
you sent prophets to set us right.
You pulled down the arrogant   *Luke 1:52*
and lifted up the weak.
And when the time was right, you sent Jesus   *Gal. 4:4*
to set us free.

Now send us again your life-giving Spirit
and recharge your promise within us,
for we are eagerly awaiting our Savior   *Phil. 3:20*
to come again from heaven.

Holy, holy, holy, God of power and might,
heaven and earth are full of your glory.
Hosanna in the highest.
Blessed is the One who comes in the name of our God.
Hosanna in the highest!

So with gratitude and expectation
we remember that Jesus took bread,
blessed, broke, and gave it
to his disciples, saying,
This is my body, given for you.

So also we remember
that Jesus took the cup, saying,
This is the new covenant of love and grace
poured out for you and for many.   *Matt. 26:28*
Do this in remembrance of me.

Now, as we wait for him to come again, O God,
stir up your power and restore us   *Ps. 80:2–3*
by sending your Holy Spirit
to infuse us with hope
in the great mystery of our faith:
Christ has died,
Christ is risen,
Christ will come again.

All glory and honor are yours,
eternal God,
through Christ, with Christ, in Christ,
in the unity of the Holy Spirit,
now and forever. **Amen.**

CHRISTMAS EVE

INVITATION TO THE TABLE
Long ago, the glory of God
in fire and cloud
was so great
that God said to Moses,
"You cannot see my face;
for no one shall see me and live."   *Exod. 33:20*
To this day, no one has ever seen God.   *John 1:18*
Yet, the astonishment of Christmas is this:
Immanuel, God-with-us, was born
and lived among us,
face to face.
In him we have seen God's glory
—full of grace and truth.   *John 1:14*
Not only on a high mountain,
but here at the Table,
he has promised to meet us,
in bread broken and cup poured out.
From his fullness we have all received,   *John 1:16*
grace upon grace.

THE GREAT PRAYER OF THANKSGIVING
The Lord be with you.
And also with you.
Lift up your hearts.
We lift them to the Lord.
Let us give thanks to the Lord our God.
It is right to give our thanks and praise.

Creator God, we give you thanks and praise
for the beauty of the earth in every season.
Especially we thank you for the beauty in this season
    of Christmas.
The stars of night light our way,
just as Jesus the true light
reveals to us the way of life.
Trees and branches,
fruits and berries and flowers
overflow with reminders of your great abundance
toward us in creation.
As Christmas is celebrated in snow and heat,
in dry desert and tropical forest,
each climate praises
the diversity of your design.

Even with all you have done for us,
we turned against you,
rejecting your love.
Yet you did not stop loving us.
Instead, you sent prophets,   *Isa. 52:7*
messengers who announced peace,
good news,
salvation!
Therefore we break forth together into singing: *Isa. 52:9*
Holy, holy, holy Lord, God of power and might,
heaven and earth are full of your glory.
Hosanna in the highest.
Blessed is he who comes in the name of the Lord.
Hosanna in the highest.

As you spoke long ago to our ancestors   *Heb. 1:1–4*
in many and various ways,
you have spoken to us by a Son,
Jesus Christ.
He is the reflection of your glory;
the exact imprint of your very being;
and all things are sustained by his powerful word.
He lived among us, died for us,
and now sits at the right hand of Majesty on high.

We thank you that on the night before he died,
Jesus took bread
and, giving thanks to you,
broke it, and gave it to his disciples, saying:
Take, eat.
This is my body, given for you.
Do this in remembrance of me.
Then he also took the cup, saying:
This cup is the new covenant sealed in my blood,
shed for you for the forgiveness of sins.
Whenever you drink it,
do this in remembrance of me.

Celebrating these gifts from our Savior,
we speak the mystery of faith:
Christ has died.
Christ is risen.
Christ will come again.

Gracious God, pour out your Holy Spirit upon us
and upon this bread and wine,
joining us in true communion with Christ
and with all who share this feast,
in heaven and on earth.
May we truly receive him,   *John 1:12–13*
and so believe in his name,
that we have power to become children of God,
united in ministry in every place.

Through Christ, with Christ, in Christ,
in the unity of the Holy Spirit,
all glory belongs to you, O God,
full of grace and truth. **Amen.**

EPIPHANY

The Lord be with you.
And also with you.
Lift up your hearts.
We lift them to the Lord.
Let us give thanks to the Lord our God.
It is right to give our thanks and praise.

It is a right and joyful thing to offer thanks to you, O God,
the source of all creation.
Your holy energy flows in animals and plants,
makes them move,
and gives them desire to live.
You brought forth the world in love,
and in your great love creation finds at last its proper end.
And so with the hosts of heaven
we join the everlasting hymn of praise:

Holy, holy, holy Lord, God of power and might.
Heaven and earth are full of your glory.
Hosanna in the highest.
Blessed is he who comes in the name of the Lord.
Hosanna in the highest.

You fill our world with glory and light,
and yet our mortal eyes cannot behold so bright a truth.
Therefore in time you sent us Jesus Christ,
your truth made flesh.

He lived among us, teaching, healing,
and revealing the boundless riches of your grace,
that everyone might see and know the power of your
    love for us.   *Eph. 3:8–9*
[For on the night he was betrayed the Lord took bread,
and giving thanks and breaking it, he said,
"This is my body, given for you."
And after supper he took the cup, and giving thanks,
    he said,
"This is my blood of the covenant, which is poured out
    for many."]   *Mark 14:22–24*

Remembering the life and work of Christ,
his ministry among the poor and lost,
his death upon the cross of human shame,
and the victory revealed by the empty tomb,
we offer you our lives in thanks and praise,
in unity with Christ our friend and Lord.
Send your Holy Spirit on us here
and on the gifts of bread and wine we share.
Make us, gathered here in love for you,
members of the body of our Lord,
that we may share the promise of the gospel,   *Eph. 3:6*
one with Christ, and one in ministry to all the world.
Through Christ and in the power of the Holy Spirit,
all glory and honor are yours,
Almighty God, now and forever. **Amen.**

TRANSFIGURATION OF THE LORD

The Lord be with you.
And also with you.
Lift up your hearts.
We lift them to the Lord.
Let us give thanks to the Lord our God.
It is right to give our thanks and praise.

Mighty God of Moses and Elijah,
you come to us in a whirlwind of mystery,
a swirling tempest, a devouring fire.

Yet you come to us—
speaking faithfulness and mercy,
shining light in our darkness,
offering forgiveness for our sin.

Therefore we praise you,
joining the hymn of the six-winged seraphs,
who cover their faces as they sing:

Holy, holy, holy Lord, God of power and might,
heaven and earth are full of your glory.
Hosanna in the highest.
Blessed is he who comes in the name of the Lord.
Hosanna in the highest.

We give you thanks for Jesus Christ,
the light of the world—
shining at the dawn of creation,
shining in our hearts this day
with a splendor that overshadows
all the beauty of heaven and earth.

In his face we have seen your glory;
through his words we have heard your truth;
by his living and dying and rising
we have come to know
the height and breadth and depth
of your great love.

With thanksgiving, we remember
the bread of life—
taken, blessed, broken, and given
that we might be holy and whole.

With thanksgiving, we remember
the cup of salvation—
your new covenant of grace,
poured out in love for the world.

Remembering your faithfulness and mercy
as we share this bread and cup,
we offer ourselves in your service
through Jesus Christ our Lord.

Great is the mystery of faith:
Christ has died,
Christ is risen,
Christ will come again.

Now let us share in your Holy Spirit—
poured out in this place,
for these people,
upon this bread and cup.

By your Spirit, make us one people—
one in the promise of Moses,
one in the prophecy of Elijah,
as we seek to proclaim the gospel
of Jesus Christ our Lord.

Let our lives shine with Christ's light—
a blessing of joy to the living,
a beacon of hope to the dying,
the dawning of a new creation.

All this we pray to you, O God,
through the gift of your Spirit
and in the grace of your Word,
to the glory of your holy name. **Amen.**

LENT

The Lord be with you.
And also with you.
Lift up your hearts.
We lift them to the Lord.
Let us give thanks to the Lord our God.
It is right to give our thanks and praise.

It is truly right and our greatest joy
to give you thanks, Creator God,
for you made the world and all that is in it.
You called us into relationship with you,
providing all we need for abundant life.
Yet we turned away,
violating our relationship with you
and acting with violence toward one another
and all creation.
Yet you did not reject us
but continued to reach out and restore us.
Over and over again,
you have made covenant to be our God,
calling us to be your faithful people.
We give thanks for signs of your covenantal love:
you put your bow in the cloud,   *Gen. 9:13–17*
a unilateral promise never to destroy the earth
     in anger again.
You pointed to the night sky,
promising Abraham and Sarah a son   *Gen. 17:1–7, 15–16*

and descendants to outnumber the stars
    in the heavens.
As your covenantal love continued,
you gave us commandments carved in stone   *Exod. 20:1–17*
so that we might know how to live faithfully
with you and one another.
Through the prophet Jeremiah,
you promised to make still a new covenant with us,   *Jer. 31:31–34*
one written on our very hearts.

Therefore we praise you
for your great mercy and steadfast love.
With the faithful of every time and place,
we sing to the glory of your name:

Holy, holy, holy Lord, God of power and might,
heaven and earth are full of your glory.
Hosanna in the highest.
Blessed is he who comes in the name of the Lord.
Hosanna in the highest.

You are holy, Lord of hosts,
and blessed is Jesus Christ, your Son, our Savior.
You sent him into the world,
calling us to repent   *Mark 1:15*
and to welcome the kingdom you bring.
Tempted in every way as we are,   *Mark 1:12–13*
he never sinned.
Instead, he turned away from violence,
teaching us the way of peace.
He rejected power that corrupts,
choosing instead to live as a servant among us.
He did not turn stones into easy bread   *Matt. 4:3–4*
but instead offered us the bread of life—
justice, freedom,
health, unconditional love—
so that we might never be hungry again.
Showing the depth of your love,
he offered us the cup of the new covenant,   *Matt. 26:28*
sealed in his blood.

We give thanks that the Lord Jesus,
on the night before he died,
took bread,
and, after giving thanks to you,
broke it, and gave it to his disciples, saying,
Take, eat.
This is my body, given for you.
Do this in remembrance of me.

In the same way he took the cup, saying,
This cup is the new covenant sealed in my blood,
shed for you for the forgiveness of sins.
Whenever you drink it,
do this in remembrance of me.

In this Lenten season,
we rejoice that we share in his baptism,
in his dying and rising again,
and we look with hope for the kingdom of God in its fullness.
Great is the mystery of faith:
Christ has died,
Christ is risen,
Christ will come again.

Gracious God,
as your Spirit hovered over creation, *Gen. 1:2*
as your Spirit descended like a dove on Jesus, *Mark 1:10–11*
your beloved Son,
may your Spirit now hover over us,
and descend on us and these your gifts of bread and wine,
that the bread we break
and the cup we bless
may be the communion of the body and blood of Christ.
By your Spirit, make us one with Christ,
and one with all who share this feast.
Bind us in covenantal love to you
and to one another in the church,
that we may reach out to the world
with justice, freedom,

health, and unconditional love
in Christ's name,
until the promised day of your kingdom.

Through Christ, with Christ, in Christ,
in the unity of the Holy Spirit,
all glory and honor are yours, almighty God,
now and forever. **Amen.**

PALM SUNDAY / PASSION SUNDAY

The Lord be with you.
And also with you.
Lift up your hearts.
We lift them up to God.
Let us give thanks to the Lord our God.
It is right to give our thanks and praise.

We praise you, O God, source of all creation,
for the mighty work of love
by which you redeemed us in Christ.
To you be praise and dominion forever.

You sent your Son Jesus for the healing of the world
that we might learn to follow his life of humility
and share in the joy of his glorious resurrection.
And so we praise you as we say:

Holy, holy, holy Lord, God of power and might,
Heaven and earth are full of your glory.
Hosanna in the highest.
Blessed is the One who comes in the name of the Lord.
Hosanna in the highest.

On the night before he died for us,
Jesus gathered his friends for a meal.
He took bread, gave you thanks, broke it,
gave it to them, and said,

Take, eat, this is my body,
which is given for you;
do this in remembrance of me.

After supper he took the cup;
when he had given thanks,
he gave it to them and said,
This cup is the new covenant in my blood,
poured out for the forgiveness of sins;
do this in remembrance of me.
Christ has died,
Christ has risen,
Christ will come in glory.

Remembering his cross and resurrection,
where all that was lost is now restored,
we offer you our praise and thanks.
Send your Holy Spirit upon our celebration,
that we may be fed with the body and blood of your Son
and be filled with your grace.

Unite us with Christ in his suffering
that we may also know his glory,
and strengthen us to reveal your justice,
until all are made whole again
in your kingdom without end.

All this we pray through your Son,
Jesus Christ our Savior,
who with you and the Holy Spirit
lives and reigns now and forever. **Amen.**

HOLY THURSDAY

INVITATION TO THE TABLE

    Friends, this is the Table of the Lord.
    From the night of his arrest through
        succeeding generations,
    Jesus' disciples have continued to come to the Table
        for this holy meal.
    As he did that night in Jerusalem,
    so ever since in all times and places,
    Christ meets us here.
    We are included in this feast,
    whether we are filled with faith or emptied by doubt;
    whether we are first among saints, last among scoundrels,
    or somewhere in between.
    In bread broken and cup poured out,
    we remember the full extent of Christ's love for us   *John 13:1b*
    and give thanks.
[or]
    As early as the year 50 AD [or CE],
    the apostle Paul wrote this to the congregation
        in Corinth: *1 Cor. 11:23–26*
    I received from the Lord what I also handed
        on to you,
    that the Lord Jesus on the night when he
        was betrayed
    took bread, and when he had
        given thanks,
    he broke it and said,
    "This is my body that is for you.
    Do this in remembrance of me."

After supper, he took the cup also, saying,
"This cup is the new covenant in my blood.
Do this in remembrance of me."
For as often as you eat this bread and drink the cup,
you proclaim the Lord's death until he comes.

The significance of this night
has been kept by the church
from earliest years.
Tonight, this sacrament is once again handed on to us
    in our generation.

Come, let us join the whole communion of saints
as we keep the feast!

THE GREAT PRAYER OF THANKSGIVING

The Lord be with you.
And also with you.
Lift up your hearts.
We lift them to the Lord.
Let us give thanks to the Lord our God.
It is right to give our thanks and praise.

It is right, Creator and Ruler of the Universe,
to give you thanks and praise.
You formed the world and called it good.
In the days of Noah,
when humankind had become thoroughly evil   *Gen. 6:5*
in thought and deed,
you sent the great flood to destroy all that you had made.
Yet, in mercy,
you caused the ark to float in safety.
Then, on dry ground, Noah and his family,   *Gen. 7–8*
and living creatures of every kind,
were brought out by you to begin again.
Beginning with Abraham,   *Gen. 12:1–4*
you formed a people as your own
and made covenant to be their God.
When we were slaves in Egypt,
you heard our cries,   *Exod. 2:23–25*
sending Moses to lead us into freedom.

You parted the waters of the sea,   *Exod. 14:15–16*
leading Israel safely through on dry ground.
Though you gave us the promised land
and made of us a great nation,
we continued to turn from your ways and betray
    your commands.
Yet, in love and enduring mercy,
you continued to call us back to you
through the words of the prophets.
We now call out to you,
forever praising your steadfast love and glory:

Holy, holy, holy Lord, God of power and might,
heaven and earth are full of your glory.
Hosanna in the highest.
Blessed is the One who comes in the name of the Lord.
Hosanna in the highest.

You are holy, O God of glory,
and blessed is Jesus Christ, your Son, our Lord.
He lived among us,
teaching and healing,
gathering the outcast and the sinner,
welcoming everyone into the way of abundant life.
By serving, he taught us how to serve.
By loving us fully,
he gave the example of how we are to love one another.
Even on the night of his betrayal,
he loved his own to the end.

[If they have not already been said, the words of institution may be said
here or in relation to the breaking of bread, using the text given above,
from 1 Cor. 11:23–26.]

Remembering all your mighty and merciful acts,
we take this bread and this wine,
gifts from the earth,
and celebrate with thanksgiving
the saving love of Jesus Christ.
Accept, we pray, this offering of thanksgiving,
as we proclaim the one crucified and risen.

Great is the mystery of faith:
Christ has died,
Christ is risen,
Christ will come again.

Gracious God,
pour out your Holy Spirit upon us
and upon this bread and wine,
that the bread we break
and the cup we bless
may be for us the communion of the body and blood of Christ.
By your Spirit, bind us in love
to the church of every time and place.
Loving one another,
may we bear witness that we are disciples of Christ
and serve others as he served us.
With our whole bodies—head, hands, feet—
we give ourselves in humility and gratitude
as we await the day
when we will share this feast at your table in glory.

Through Christ, with Christ, in Christ,
in the unity of the Holy Spirit,
all glory and honor are yours, eternal God,
now and forever. **Amen.**

PRAYER AFTER COMMUNION
O Lord our God,
we rise from this table
knowing a love beyond our deserving.
Thank you for giving us a place at your table;
for serving us the bread of life;
for offering to us,
even to us,
the cup of salvation.
In humility and hope,
we go now from this night
to your promised day.
In Christ we pray. **Amen.**

EASTER

The Lord be with you.
And also with you.
Lift up your hearts.
We lift them to the Lord.
Let us give thanks to the Lord our God.
It is right to give our thanks and praise.

In every time and every age, O God,
it is good and faithful that we give you thanks,
for your mercy is sure
and your steadfast love endures forever.   *Ps. 118:2*
In your compassion you gave us Christ Jesus,
who frees us from darkness
and lights our path to endless renewal and life eternal.
And so, with all of creation,
with all the needy and hungry ones,
with all those who have enough and plenty,
with creatures large and small,
with sun and moon and stars,
and with the saints of every age,
we praise your name and join their unending hymn:

Holy, holy, holy Lord, God of power and might,
heaven and earth are full of your glory.
Hosanna in the highest.
Blessed is he who comes in the name of the Lord.
Hosanna in the highest.

Blessed are you, O God, creator of all things.
By your power and love you continue
to deliver your people from bondage,
thwart the designs of evil,
show the way through the wilderness,
turn hardship into righteousness,
and reveal your hand upholding the just.

Blessed are you, O Christ, servant of the universe.
You came among us to feed and heal and teach,
to confound the haughty,
to confuse the tricksters,
to challenge the wrong-hearted,
and, in all these things,
to give hope to those who long for peace.

We remember that on the night he was betrayed,
having gathered his friends at the table,
our Lord Jesus took bread and gave thanks,
broke it, and gave it to his disciples, saying:
Take and eat. This is my body given for you.
Do this for the remembrance of me.

And again, after supper, he took the cup
and gave it for all to drink, saying:
This cup is the new covenant in my blood
shed for you and for all people
for the forgiveness of sin.
Do this for the remembrance of me.

Remembering our Lord's self-giving love,
we proclaim the mystery of faith:
Christ has died.
Christ has risen.
Christ will come again.

Blessed are you, O Spirit, giver of life.
You give us words when we have none;
you fill us with vision when we have the most need;
you give us voice to proclaim our faith in every hour.
Be our guide and teacher, today and always.

Come now, O Prince of Peace,
Spirit of Love,
Breath of Life.
Bring to all this hurting world the joy that Mary knew,
and teach us to proclaim with her,
"I have seen the Lord!"   *John 20:18*
In the unity of the Holy Trinity,
in gratitude for this great day of resurrection,
we praise you, God of all that is,
now and forever. **Amen.**

ASCENSION OF THE LORD

The Lord be with you.
And also with you.
Lift up your hearts.
We lift them to the Lord.
Let us give thanks to the Lord our God.
It is right to give our thanks and praise.

It is a right and joyful thing to offer thanks to you,
God of wisdom and hope.
In every age you have confirmed in the saints
     your glorious inheritance
and the immeasurable greatness of your power
among those who put their trust in you.   *Eph. 1:18–19*
And so with angels and archangels and
     all the host of heaven,
we sing your praise and join the everlasting hymn:

Holy, holy, holy Lord, God of power and might.
Heaven and earth are full of your glory.
Hosanna in the highest.
Blessed is he who comes in the name of the Lord.
Hosanna in the highest.

Blessed are you and blessed is your Son, Jesus Christ.
You revealed your life-giving power through Christ
and raised him from the dead to sit at your right hand
     in glory,
far above every rule and authority of heaven and earth.   *Eph. 1:20–21*

And yet he lived among us, our friend and brother,
offering himself for our salvation.
For on the night he was betrayed, Jesus took bread,
and giving thanks and breaking it, he said,
This is my body given for you.
And after supper he took the cup, and giving thanks, he said,
This is my blood of the covenant, which is poured out for many.

O God, because we remember the life and work of Christ,
his ministry among the poor and forsaken,
his death upon the cross of human shame,
the victory of the empty tomb,
and his ascension to glory,
we offer our lives in praise and thanksgiving
to be a living sacrifice in union with Christ our Lord.

Send your Holy Spirit on us gathered here
and on the gifts of bread and wine we share.
Let them be our communion with Christ, who dwells
    with you in glory.
Through our communion, make us members of his body,
    united in love,
that we may be Christ for the world
and manifest the fullness of him who fills all in all.   *Eph. 1:23*
Through Christ, in the power of the Holy Spirit,
glory and honor are yours,
Almighty God, now and forever. **Amen.**

DAY OF PENTECOST

The Lord be with you.
And also with you.
Lift up your hearts.
We lift them to the Lord.
Let us give thanks to the Lord our God.
It is right to give our thanks and praise.

It is always good that we give you thanks, O God,
for you sent your Holy Spirit into our midst,
the Spirit of wisdom and might,
who brings us into communion with you and with one another.
And so, with all the people of God in every age,
we praise you for the power of the resurrection
to set us free from divisions and strife,
and with angels and archangels,
with earth, water, fire, and air,
and with all your creatures,
we praise your name and join their unending hymn:

Holy, holy, holy Lord, God of power and might,
heaven and earth are full of your glory.
Hosanna in the highest.
Blessed is he who comes in the name of the Lord.
Hosanna in the highest.

Blessed are you, O God,
by whose word all things came into being,
whose power brings the dead to life,
whose breath undergirds our prayers,

and whose love for rich diversity
amazes and astonishes your people.

Blessed are you, O Christ, Word made flesh,
who came to us as prophet, brother, and savior.
We thank you for your life among the multitudes,
preaching, teaching, feeding, healing,
lifting up the ones who falter
and calling the powerful to righteousness.

We remember that on the night he was betrayed,
having gathered his friends at the table,
our Lord Jesus took bread and gave thanks,
broke it, and gave it to his disciples, saying:
Take and eat. This is my body given for you.
Do this for the remembrance of me.

And again, after supper, he took the cup
and gave it for all to drink, saying:
This cup is the new covenant in my blood
shed for you and for all people
for the forgiveness of sin.
Do this for the remembrance of me.

Remembering our Lord's command
to remember him, his wisdom, and his sacrifice,
we proclaim the mystery of faith:
Christ has died.
Christ has risen.
Christ will come again.

Blessed are you, O Spirit,
poured out upon your people
to open our hearts,
to pray within us,
to teach us hope.

Through this broken bread, show us life abundant.
Break us, as well, so that with your gifts,
we may tend your earth and feed the hungry,
giving thanks for all that nourishes
this blessed creation, now and forever. **Amen.**

Scripture Index